Altitude or Attitude

A Geek's Travel Log

San Francisco to Concordia-K2-Gondogoro La of Pakistan

Ifti Mirza

DEDICATION

Dedicated to my family and friends who laugh at my jokes, listen to my stories, and love me unconditionally. I love you back and more. You know who you are.

CONTENTS

CONTENTS

ACKNOWLEDGMENTS

Thank you to my many friends who have encouraged me throughout, either by proofreading or by cheerleading. You rock! Thanks to Marcy Timberman, a very good friend of mine, for diligently reviewing each line of the book. A very special thanks to Nouman Khan, of TDCP (Tourism Development Corporation of Punjab), Pakistan, for going through full content and providing technical feedback. Many thanks to Josh Higham, Masood Siddiqi, and Reshma Hyder for the book review and their excellent suggestions. Thanks to Azmi Gill of Urdu News for continuous feedback, and for my wife Farah, to get me started on writing this book and to make sure I complete it. Also thanks to my K2 team; Kashif Rafique, Asim Mirza, Salman Zakir, Nauman Siddiqui, Ahtisham Ahmad, Saad Munawar, Nouman Khan, Wazir Afzal and Munna Ibrahim for their company on an incredible and unforgettable journey.

1

THE BUG

It's been quite some time since I have taken a flight out of Pakistan to make a living. I am hitting twenty years of being an overseas Pakistani. I have been living in San Francisco Bay Area, also known to the world as Silicon Valley to the world, for some time now. I never knew that I would call San Francisco Bay Area my home. San Francisco was way too far away and way out of my league for me to even think about back when I was in Pakistan.

This year I wanted to connect to myself at a deeper level. We are creatures of nature, and we belong to nature, and we will disappear into nature as many of us already have. I wanted more space than just the few hours here and there. I wanted to connect with nature, and nothing was better than starting from my backyard. I am blessed to have two countries that I can call home. One country where I was born and raised, where I learned to crawl, walk and then run, where I was given unconditional love and where I fell in love with reading. The other country where I was accepted and welcomed unconditionally, where I learned a lot, a country which taught me to be me, a country where my kids are born, where I am respected based on my skills, not color. A country which gave me opportunities to meet people from different beautiful cultures thus giving me many perspectives on life. A country where I was able to make friends from around the globe without actually traveling.

Back in the days in Pakistan, while strolling through a bookstore I saw a postcard with a picture of some tents pitched in front of the massive snowy magical mountain. That particular postcard for some reasons triggered a bug in me and made me promise myself that if that mountain happens to be in Pakistan, I would go there by any means, no matter what. Lo, and behold that place turned out to be Fairy Meadows at Nanga Parbat in Pakistan Himalayas. Upon some little research I found out that Nanga Parbat was the ninth highest peak of the world and it reached as high as 26,660 feet (8,126 meters). I was ecstatic. I got fixated on it, and every time I thought about Nanga Parbat I would feel different. A low voltage would go through my body giving me enough jolt to make me feel alive. It was on me to fulfill the promise that I made myself.

Long story short eventually I was able to trek to Nanga Parbat despite many failed attempts. It was unfathomable that such a beauty, Nanga Parbat, was hidden behind such a remote, rugged monstrous terrain. I recall that, once I made it, I was truly awestruck by the beauty of the majestic Nanga Parbat and magical Fairy Meadows back then. It was hard to achieve what I accomplished with limited experience and tight resources, but I never realized that I was creating lifetime memories. It was that bug that carried me through that ordeal and only a few could understand. I guess this was when I indirectly infected a couple of my friends with the bug. They saw my pics and listened to my stories and got hooked.

I have been away from home for so long that I am usually criticized by my friends and family that I have fallen for the bright lights of the West and its material race. One thing that they probably don't understand is what sets the West apart from others, is the West's love for nature. Especially in the U.S where national parks are the world's natural treasure troves. I have been to many national parks in the U.S. and the way that people in the U.S. protect their parks is very heartening and worthy of praise. One should not underestimate the beauty these parks have within their gates and boundaries.

Out of the two backyards that I call home, this year I decided to go to Pakistan exclusively for trekking and out of all treks in Pakistan, there is no Trek better than Concordia Trek which takes one to footsteps of K-2 peak hidden in rugged Karakoram mountain range.

Why K2 and Concordia

K2, the beauty, and the beast, is the second highest mountain in the world. It sits high and proud in the remote Karakoram Mountain range at the northern tip of Pakistan close to China. K2, just 800 feet shy of the world's highest mountain, Mount Everest, is regarded as one of the most dangerous mountains to climb. So far, there have been 300 summits and 77 fatalities. One climber has died for each four climbers who have successfully put their feet on its peak. Hence K2 is also called Savage Mountain. Unlike other mountains, which are of the K2 League, mostly eight-thousanders, K2 has never been summited in winter. Eight-thousanders are the peaks over 8,000 meters (26,246 ft.) and higher. Eight-thousanders are a handful in our planet, total fourteen in the world, five of which are in Pakistan

K2 is also accessible from China side, but that side is extremely dangerous thus most of the attempts are made from Pakistan side. K2 at 8,611 meters (28,251 ft.) above sea level, at first glance, looks like a frozen pyramid with exposed cliffs. It is a consistently steep pyramid, dropping quickly in almost all directions. It stands over 3,000 meters (9,840 ft.) above much of the glacial valley bottoms at its base. The north side is the steepest: there it rises over 3,200 meters (10,500 ft.) above the K2 (Qogir) Glacier in only 3,000 meters (9,800 ft.) of horizontal distance. In most directions, it achieves over 2,800 meters (9,200 ft.) of vertical relief in less than 4,000 meters (13,000 ft.).

In 1856, a European team first surveyed the mountain K-2. Team member Thomas Montgomerie designated the mountain "K-2" for being the second peak of the Karakoram range. The other peaks were initially named K1, K3, K4, and K5, but were eventually renamed to Masherbrum, Gasherbrum IV, Gasherbrum II, and Gasherbrum I, respectively. In 1892, Martin Conway led a British expedition that reached "Concordia" on the Baltoro Glacier.

An Italian expedition finally succeeded in ascending to the summit of K2 via the Abruzzi Spur on 31 July 1954. On 9 August 1977, Ichiro Yoshizawa of Japan, led the second successful ascent, with Ashraf Aman as the first native Pakistani climber. The Japanese expedition took the Abruzzi Spur and used more than 1,500 porters. On 26 July 2014, the first team of Pakistani climbers scaled K2. There were six Pakistani and three Italian climbers in the expedition, called K2 60 Years Later, according to BBC. Previously, K2 had only been summited by individual Pakistanis as part of international teams. On 27

ALTITUDE OR ATTITUDE

July 2014, Garrett Madison led a team of three American climbers and six Sherpas to summit K2. At the time of this writing, K2 has not been summited since 2014. One of the challenges that the K2 expeditions still face is to reach its base camp. Even to this day, it takes at least seven days of trekking to get to the base camp from the last town accessible by jeep. I have always been fascinated by K2. It had always been my dream to be at K2 and this year I wanted to do something about it. I am not getting younger, so I thought I should at least go to K2 basecamp, if not the climb. Climbing K2 is way out of the league for me for now. The trek that takes one to K2 basecamp is known as Concordia Trek.

Concordia is the name for the confluence of the mighty Baltoro Glacier, the Godwin-Austen Glacier, and Vigne Glacier, in the heart of the Karakoram range in Pakistan. It is located in Baltistan region of Pakistan. The name was applied by European explorers, and comes from this location's similarity to a glacial confluence, also called Concordia, in the Bernese Oberland, part of the Central Alps. Concordia offers the region's best place to camp for mountain enthusiasts not involved in climbing. With scenic views, it also provides short treks to several important base camps: K2 (five to six hours of trekking), Broad Peak (two to three hours of trekking) and the Gasherbrum I & II (seven to eight hours of trekking). An alternative exit to returning down the Baltoro Glacier is available by climbing the Gondogoro La 18,500 feet (5615 meters).

I will not tell you how many people have died even going to the foothills of K2, rather I will tell you how it feels like to be there, how it feels when you prepare for such a journey and how it feels when you return. I will introduce you to the many characters that I met on the trek, some of which are great friends now and some have disappeared into memory lane. I will tell you about the ins and outs of the daily routine. I want you to come with me, feel the pain, feel the suffering, and feel the joy. I want you to walk on glaciers with me, jump over the crevasses, tie ropes, climb, and rappel down. I guarantee that it will be an out of the world experience.

Getting Things Rolling

In summer of 2015, I started pinging my old-timer friend, who lives in Islamabad, the green capitol of Pakistan. I kept harassing him by pinging messages such as "There?" and "*Kiddan* (there, in the Punjabi language)" every once in a while. I finally got a response from him on December 1st: "Yes bro, *hukum* (what's up, in the Urdu language)"? I then posed him the question "K2 coming August *Inshallah*, you ready?" and he responded "*Inshallah*." Inshallah, an Arabic expression, literally means "Allah willing.". But in practice, it implies that God could be willing, but I may or may not be willing. I knew I had my foot in the door and I just needed to push more to get things going. I kept pinging him every other month and then finally in May of 2016 we talked on the phone regarding dates and details of the trek. Concordia was a trek that we had always dreamt of but never dared of even thinking about doing it. Once I got semi-confirmation from him, I called up another good old friend of mine in Pakistan and asked him if he was up for it. The good friend of twenty plus years didn't even bother asking what the plans were. He just said yes.

After opening up talk with my old friend, who is also my distant relative from the obscure town DG Khan of South Punjab and now living in capital city Islamabad, I knew I needed to get things rolling. Before I could even start preparing, I needed to get the travel dates and secure an air ticket for San Francisco to Islamabad trip. Pakistan is far from the U.S., but travel time and weather change are not the only barriers. One needs to consider the cost as well. Tickets start at $2,000 in the season, and it is always the season when you are traveling. You may get the ticket for $1,700-$1,800 if you pick mid-week departure and arrival dates for your flights. Before I could embark on such trip, I needed to secure the airline ticket within the reasonable budget and within the dates that are best for Concordia trek and with enough money left over to purchase the equipment required for the trek and the money required while in Pakistan.

There is a limited time window for the trekking at such altitude, and within that window, there are occasions, which are better than others. Concordia trek starts at approximately 10,000 feet and goes up to approximately 16,500 feet and if you are up for more adventure you can go up to 19,000 feet. Weather can quickly tilt your trip from happening to not happening.

We figured that the best would be the last two weeks of July. The various guidebooks suggest that mid-July to mid-August is the best season. We have the option to go as a small team and arrange for porters and food on our own. Going as a small team could be a hassle and can quickly turn into a nightmare. Another option was to use services of a tour operator that can reduce the headache of day-to-day hustling. A reliable tour operator can guarantee the right resources at the right time. For example, if you need a jeep ride on a specific day, then you really want that jeep to show up. Otherwise, you could spend days waiting. If you run out of supplies or suffer losses due to the theft, damage or mistakes, or you have some communication issues with your logistics, then it could put you in a precarious situation. Resources such as transportation, lodging, and food are not abundant due to remoteness and ruggedness of the area. You cannot shop around there.

There is no electricity and no cell towers, and you will not be going through towns to replenish your stocks. Once you are out there, you are out there. Some regional economic gaps have created some local rules that you would only know once you are there. Some villages require you to hire porters or services from them. I believe it's mainly to encourage local economy. It will not be wise to show up with all resources, especially the labor, and walk past the villages. There is also competition among communities. These are remote villages; they survive on livestock and fields where they grow their wheat, vegetables, and fruit. Trekkers and adventurers provide them with a welcome income that now many families depend upon.

Based on word-of-mouth recommendations, we engaged a tour company that was led by a person who was from a small remote village known as Hushe. The Hushe village is known for producing world-class mountaineers. Hushe has hardworking, passionate mountaineers who have built their reputation as world-class climbers and high altitude porters by their sheer willpower and ingenuity.

Once we finalized on a tour operator who met our requirements, the ball was in my court to procure the air ticket, arrange for the required equipment, and work out our schedule with the tour company. I estimated I would need four weeks to pull off this trip. Luckily I have not taken a day off for some time, and I was able to get my vacation approved by my company.

I spent hours and hours online looking for an air ticket, and it was becoming quite frustrating. Air ticket prices were like stock trades. Prices fluctuate a lot and it got my head spinning. I was not getting a reasonable ticket price, and at one point it looked like I would have to let go of this trip. In my online ticket purchasing effort, I expanded my search for the flights on United Airlines website. I happened to have United credit card which came with some bonus miles. While I almost gave up on searching I saw an excellent deal on United Airlines website, and I sealed it. Flight connections were odd and there were extra-long layovers to my travel, but at least it would take me to where I wanted to go and hopefully would bring me back in one piece and on promised time.

Chance Favors the Prepared Mind

Once the air ticket was out of the way, I turned my focus on my equipment checklist. Other than the items on one's list, one need to be conscious of one's physical fitness. The desire to be at K2 base camp is very commendable but lacking in physical fitness could be dangerous. Friends have asked that how fit one should be even to consider going to K2 base camp. I told that anyone who is reasonably active and has true grit would be able to do it but more fit you are more you will enjoy. You can be miserable and still do the trek but it's not advisable, and it's not fun for sure.

I have seen a hiker drop dead on Mission Peak trail in San Francisco Bay Area. The Mission Peak trail is a heavy traffic, moderate hike of 5.5 miles with an ascent of approximately 2,000 feet. Emergency medical response team arrived promptly, and there was an airlift rescue, but the hiker was gone for good, right on the trail. I later found out in the news that hiker had a heart condition. I presumed hiker's heart couldn't take the stress of the physical strain caused by hiking. And as my last and critical task, I called up the travel clinic at my local hospital. I got my Polio vaccination along with the evidence as required by Pakistan and hepatitis A vaccination as Hepatitis A has been trending in Pakistan as per hospital's travel database. I got some additional medications that included antibiotics for diarrhea and medicines for altitude sickness prevention. The hospital had very comprehensive info on diseases trends and needed vaccinations, so I strongly recommend paying a visit to your travel nurse for your international travel.

I was planning to create memories, so I purchased lightweight GoPro Session 4 camera. My destination was a photographer's paradise, but I am not a photographer and did not want the burden of a professional camera, and lenses interfere my quality time with nature. I decided my cell phone would be good enough for quick pictures and GoPro for my video diary. I threw in 15W solar panel and a battery power bank in my luggage. The solar panel was to make sure that my phone and GoPro remained charged.

Preparation could be overwhelming, but it was crucial. The more prepared you are more fun you will have. Some wise man once said that more trained you are, less you have to fight. Based on my experience and some homework, I compiled a comprehensive list of items that I thought I would need. Then I diligently worked on it to complete it.

While shopping for the shoes at an REI store, a popular store in the US specializing in outdoors equipment, I asked one of the associates if he could recommend me any shoes. I told him I will be going to K2 base camp and will be trekking on glaciers for fifteen days. I saw his eyes lit up and he exclaimed: "Wow, really?". He seemed more excited and was jubilant to help me. He then showed me "Salomon" shoes that had a price tag of $250. When he was done telling me the qualities of the shoe, I said that $250 shoe would break my budget because I have many other items to buy. He responded by saying that where I was going, he would not recommend any other shoe to me. I thanked him and walked out of the store, and he had made some valid points, but $250 was not settling in for now. I had $100-$150 in my mind for the high-quality shoe, after all, it's just trekking not professional mountaineering.

I let that settle in. The more I thought about it more it made sense to get that $250 pair of shoes. There will be no REI in Pakistan and such remote area I will not be able to buy even sandals, my only option will be to duct tape my feet if my shoes are torn apart during trekking. After few days I walked into REI again and grabbed those "Salomon" and departed $250 poorer.

I knocked off lots of items from my list but still had many critical things to work on, and by now I was way over my budget and getting frustrated. Fortunately, my co-worker and good friend had been to Nepal for trekking a year ago, and he graciously lent me his "North Face" base camp duffel bag. The yellow bag with big "North Face" logo on it turned out to be a blessing, and I was glad that I shared my plans for K2 base camp with him just in time.

Fortunately, another good friend of mine offered his equipment for me to borrow. My friend, a Stanford-educated Google engineer, was also an avid mountaineer, backpacker, and adventurer. Also, he lent me his crampons, gaiters, harness, carabiner, and glacier sunglasses. These items would have easily cost me $500 or more, so I was relieved and was appreciative of his gesture.

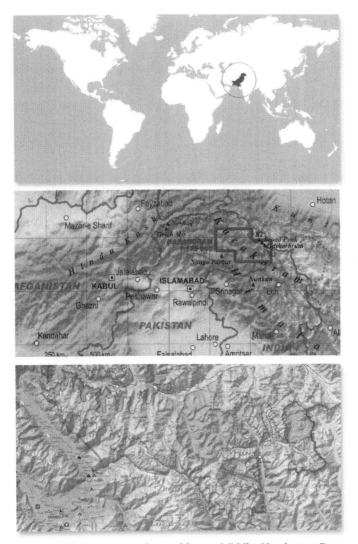

Figure 1: Top: Pakistan on the world map; Middle: Karakoram Range
Map; Bottom: Concordia Trail map; for detailed maps visit
http://www.cknp.org/cms/treks-valleys/trekking-routes/classic-treks/

13

Figure 2: Top: The K2, 8,611 meters (28,251 ft.) (photo by Salman Zakir); Bottom: Nanga Parbat, 8,126 meters (26,660 ft.)

2

SAN FRANCISCO TO ISLAMABAD VIA BEIJING

Why Beijing, you may ask? Well, when you have to travel far and save money at the same time you are left with not many options. The best economic price I got was on United Airlines from SFO to Beijing and then on Air China to Islamabad. So it was not a planned route rather forced upon one.

On the day of departure, I went through my checklist one more time, checked my gear, checked my passport, and my Pakistan National Identity Card for Overseas Pakistan (NICOP) card expiration date. I weighed my bags one more time, tucked some $100 bills and left over Pakistani currency from last year visit into my wallet and strapped my laptop bag without a laptop on my back. No laptop this time. I took a deep breath and hopped into the car. My good friend had offered the ride to the San Francisco Airport, and I gladly accepted it. No was not an option anyways. My kids and wife also tagged along. They were also excited. Farah, my wife, was concerned but told me to be careful and have fun and not worry about matters in the U.S. She had been a good sport all along. She had went through my items checklist with me and had helped me decide on some of the items and made sure that I didn't miss anything.

I knew the drill at the San Francisco International Airport. I used the self-help kiosk, but since it was international travel, document verification was required. One of the check-in staff asked if I was a U.S. citizen and if I had a visa for Pakistan. I told her that yes I was a US citizen but didn't require a visa for Pakistan as I had Pakistan national identity card, NICOP. She checked the system, took my NICOP card, punched some numbers into the system and printed out the boarding pass for Beijing. She was amazed that Pakistan still recognized me as a Pakistani citizen. She remarked that she was from Japan and the day she became US citizen, Japan had terminated her Japanese citizenship. She now had to secure Japanese visa each time she needed to visit her family in Japan. And she had never been given Japanese visa for more than thirty days. Not every country is the same, and Pakistan is better in recognizing their citizens who become citizens of other nations. I felt blessed for a moment.

I bid my farewells and proceeded to security and then to the boarding gate waiting area. I was early and not many people were there. As flight time approached boarding area started getting filled with people. The majority of the people were Chinese, and by now I felt I was already in Beijing, China. Airline professional staff handled the crowd very well, and we boarded on time and were on our way to Beijing China as per schedule. The airplane was a Boeing 747 and flight was full. The flight took off and we gained altitude.

Teh Teh

It was all my good looks and charm, that a cute girl, Chinese of course, approached and claimed the seat next to me. Not a bad start after all. It didn't take much time to start a conversation. Her name was Teh Teh and she had been in Mexico for a year for some student program and was now going to see her parent in Beijing. She had to take a connecting flight via San Francisco. There were no direct flights from Mexico to China. I guessed Chinese and Mexicans were not getting along that much.

All Chinese passengers were taking hot water for their drinks. Chinese don't drink cold water. Airline staff knew that and had plenty of warm water on that 747. Teh told me that hot water represents the warmth of one's heart to other. If someone gives you cold water, then it means that they are disrespecting you and that could mean war. I always thought Chinese are health conscious but didn't know that water temperature represented their emotional temperature. Health benefits are the bonus. Loaded with that fact, I took a mental note to serve cold water to my Chinese friends whenever I would be mad at them.

I had a good discussion with my new in-flight Chinese friend. Her name was hard to pronounce. I tried, but I was not even close. After many failed attempts of pronouncing her name, she told me her non-Chinese name, Florence. Only Chinese can pronounce Chinese names. Chinese Government officially allots an English name for a given Chinese name, go figure. I then asked Teh Teh to pronounce my name and she couldn't; now we were even.

17

Thanks to cell phone dead batteries and no in-flight entertainment we were forced to have a conversation. Teh Teh wanted to know about San Francisco, and I was trying to figure out her Mexican-Chinese connection. I found out that she had many Chinese friends in Mexico and there was good sized Chinese business community settled in Mexico. Oh well. Between her hot water and my cold water drinks, we had good conversation overall. Twelve hours flew by and we were at the Beijing Airport. Beijing welcomed us with its warm weather with a hint of humidity even though airport air-conditioners were working hard to stabilize the temperature. I said bye to Teh Teh and went my way. I followed the signs trying to figure out which line should I stand or which direction should I go. I wanted to make sure I didn't exit out the airport. There were Chinese everywhere.

Beijing Airport - Assalam o Alaikum Bhai

While I was shaking off my jet lag and trying to make sense of the signs, someone approached me and said: "Aslam o Alaikum Bhai" (May peace be on you, brother). I was surprised but reminded myself I was not in Pakistan yet. I was trying to process, but then he continued: "Bhai I need help." I thought here we go now. In my mind I imagined him as a con artist who would try to scam me by pretending that he had lost passport, money and all and now needed some money to get back to home to his little kids. Before I could final my judgement on him, I decided to talk to him more. It turned out that his brother was a Ph.D. student in South Korea and he had gone to S Korea to see his brother and now was on his way to Islamabad via Beijing. He was also trying to enroll in Master's program in South Korea, and he had recently graduated from some private Engineering college in Pakistan. He was from Swat. Swat was the scenic area that Taliban took control for some time. I was happy to see people from troubled areas making their way to higher education. Now, at Beijing Airport, he needed help to find out how to get to the flight to Islamabad. I checked his boarding pass and asked him to follow me and told him that we would be on same flight. He trailed me like a child until we made it to the boarding area for Air China flight to Islamabad. Too wipe out my guilt of judging him I bought him coffee and had a great conversation.

Still three hours to go to board the flight and it started to feel like Pakistani atmosphere. A bearded guy in *shalwar qamees* (a Pakistani traditional dress of long shirt and baggy pants, usually made from cotton) took a seat next to me and started a conversation. I must admit that my first impression was that he must be a laborer. Pakistan exports plenty of labor to Middle Eastern countries. I had also worked in Saudi Arabia as an IT (information technology) labor and had travelled a lot between Pakistan and Saudi Arabia, so I could relate. Don't get me wrong, I had always enjoyed the company of our hardworking labor passengers but I was trying to connect the dots between labor, Beijing, and Pakistan.

It was easy getting conversation going. His name was Tariq. Tariq was an intelligent man in early 30's, had a Ph.D. in economics, and travels around the world to deliver lectures on different economic forums. He was witty and a fast talker. I was impressed. He then said he wore *shalwar qamees* on international travel on purpose even though *shalwar qamees* can easily get anyone in trouble in international travels. Remember that the Taliban and Al-Qaida, who got all the prime time on media for a decade, all wore *shalwar qamees*. Tariq's goal was to fight that stereotype. We became friends quickly. When he found out that I was coming from the U.S., he thought I was one of those privileged Pakistanis who happened to have large families settled in the U.S. I briefly told him about my background and some high-level overview of hardships and struggles that I had gone through. He was impressed and gave me a compliment that I looked too young to had such an experience.

Pakistani Chinese Students

I noticed a group of university-age Pakistani boys and girls boarding the airplane. On the flight, one gal from that group happened to sit next to me. In no time, we were having a conversation. Her name was Arkham, and she had earned a scholarship to earn management degree in China. It was her first year in Chinese education system, and she was learning Chinese to get started on her advanced education in China. In just six months she was very fluent in Chinese. When in flow, she would even speak Urdu in Chinese; she was that proficient in Chinese. Her father was an Army Ranger in Karachi and was killed in a bomb blast while fighting the terrorists few years ago. She was not allowed to see her father's dead body at the funeral. Who would be able to have a normal life after seeing their loved ones, especially their dad, literally chopped up in bits and pieces? I thanked her and her family for the sacrifices and told her how brave her father was. She certainly carried the fighter genes. Even after her father's tragic death, her family held together. She was bright, she picked up, earned the top scholarship, and was now on her way to gaining her life back with great promise.

Islamabad Pakistan

It is said that in Pakistan, you cry two times: first when you arrive and second when you leave. Islamabad is about 8,000 miles from San Francisco, and the closest direct flight had one stop and twenty-two hours travel time if you are lucky with the layover. You need to keep in mind the airport check-in time that is three hours and one hour at Islamabad for immigration and baggage collection. Given the twenty-eight hours of traveling and twelve hours of time difference, when you land at Islamabad Airport you have already lost an extra calendar day. Not to mention that your head becomes heavy with jet sound, your wallet lighter because of the fare, and your stomach upset because of high altitude. The reheated frozen food that the airline serves you does the remaining damage. According to a German research, one tends to lose sensitivity for sweet and salt by 30% at high altitude due to dryness and low pressure. To counter that airline tend to salt up and spice up their meals to please the traveler's taste buds.

Also, the weather and the water combined with hygiene's of Pakistani cooking, the moment you have your first meal, you are bound to experience upset stomach that you would remember for years to come. And then you sob and wonder why you did this to yourself. To add to this, the ultra humid hot weather of Islamabad hits you like a hammer. I gave you some insights into why you would cry the first time. Stay with me and you will know why you would cry when you leave Pakistan.

y the time Air China flight 945 landed in Islamabad, I was impressed by the people I had met, and felt that I was going to very different Pakistan this time. My sister and her three boys were at the airport to welcome me. I looked for my mother and couldn't find her and guess what, I never will. She was no longer with us, but I still look for her. Pakistan was different for me after all. The weather did hit me like a hammer, but I loved it.

I couldn't help but notice that Islamabad had improved a lot since I last visited just a year ago. Improvements were not limited to the airport. The Islamabad highway was bright lit with yellow lights and the state of the art Metro bus service was operational and was in full use. There was no dust anymore. Dust had been the norm in Islamabad in recent past due to massive construction projects. Metro bus service, few new high-rise buildings, and freeway style roads had added a modern facade to Islamabad. At my sister's house, my cute little toddler nephews were genuinely happy to have their Hot Wheels toy cars. At least, I made someone jubilant.

My Good Old Multan

Once I secured my base in Islamabad, I wasted no time and was on my way to my hometown, Multan, on a flight the next day. In Multan, my goal was to grab my friend Kashif and if possible negotiate his release from his wife and mother. Kashif had told me that he was a big boy now but I didn't want to take any chances. He was ready, and his bags were packed when I met him.

I visited my empty childhood house which was full of life not so long ago. My father and his parents had chosen Multan as their new home after India Pakistan split in 1947. My father's family migrated from India to Multan in harsh conditions and some of them lost their lives. One of elders in my family had told us that she had seen her brother's headless body on an abandoned cart but they had to leave him behind. It always gives me chills whenever thought of India Pakistan migration comes to my mind.

Multan was now a populous but a neglected town which sits at the southern tip of the Pakistan's wealthy province Punjab. In recent years, Multan had developed a bit. After assassination of Benazir Bhutto, a popular political figure in Pakistan, Yousaf Gillani of Multan being non-controversial member of Benazir's political party, became Pakistan's prime minister. Gillani personally oversaw projects for Multan's development. International's standard airport, fly over bridges, burn center, you name it. Only a geek like me would connect dots with Benazir's assassination to Multan's development.

Other reason that I visited Multan was to say hi to my mother, father, uncles, aunts, cousins and grandparents who had been resting in peace for some time under marked clay graves in a shade less dusty graveyard. Multan was ironically famous for its dust, graveyards and Sufi shrines. I never had thought my family would occupy big chunk of an unknown graveyard. I also took out time to pass through centuries old shrines of Multan, which were majestic and mystical at the same time. I have memories of sneaking in science and math books into these shrines for my exam studies. Though mostly crowded, these shrines had always provided a peaceful noiseless environments. Way more peaceful than the California's affluent Palo Alto's Mitchel library where I wrote these very sentences and many parts of this book.

After spending a day in Multan, getting back to Islamabad became somewhat of a challenge unexpectedly. The next flight was another 48 hours away, so we dumped the idea of flying. We tried our luck to get seats in a red eye bus to Islamabad. However, after getting dumped by popular bus service Daewoo in Multan, we went bus service to service with no luck. Fortunately we were able to secure tail-end seats of a next day bus. After four hours of waiting at the bus terminal and then ten hours of the bus ride, we made it to Islamabad eventually. However, we were terribly beaten up by the rough roads and the tight seats. It was a struggle reaching back to Islamabad.

Figure 3: Top left: Blue Area, Islamabad, Pakistan; Top right: A view from Monal Restaurant, Islamabad; Bottom left: Shrines of Multan, Pakistan; Bottom right: Downtown Clock Tower, Multan, Pakistan.

3

GETTING TO SKARDU

My next goal was to catch my friend Asim in Islamabad to finalize our departure and check on last minute items. Once Kashif, Asim and I were together, we charted our next steps. We went through items one more time and made sure we have all that we would need. We went last minute shopping. My friends were missing critical items such as harness, parka, waterproof pants, trekking shoes, and hat, etc.

Now, our goal was to reach Skardu. Skardu was the gateway town for Karakoram mountain range. It was the only major town in the region known as Baltistan. The population was half a million, and it was situated in the open semi-flat area near the confluence of Shigar and Indus River. Skardu was at 8,000 feet and is surrounded by gray-brown mountains. Skardu is approximately 400 miles north of Islamabad. Skardu has a small airport, and its flights are very unpredictable due to the unpredictable weather. Flight time was forty five minutes and road travel was thirty hours. It was a high season, so we decided to stick to road travel to avoid any flight cancellations scenarios.

Our Mysterious Pick Up

Friday, July 15th, Asim made some phone calls to the tour operator, and we were given a pickup point and time for the bus pickup. All our gear packed and we were at the pickup location at 6 p.m. Pick up time then got changed to 8 p.m. Our pick up point was in Blue Area Islamabad, go figure. There was nothing blue about the Blue Area. At 8 p.m., it was a dark and a deserted place.

There was a time I was intimately familiar with Blue Area of Islamabad. By the way, Blue Area was not some Islamabad's version of red light area, though in some ways it does sounds like it. It's actually a fancy boulevard with office buildings, some very high rises, on both sides stretched all the way to Pakistan's Parliament, National Assembly and Supreme Court. Some time ago, I literally went door to door to selling personally developed Inventory and Order Processing software to the offices in this very Blue Area. I was able to secure some decent contracts and a prime location in the Blue Area as an office for my software team. But that's all past now.

In that same Blue Area, under the shadows of a building where we were supposed to be picked up, we saw few random guys in a dark corner finding shelter from the rain. It turned out they were also waiting for the same pickup bus. It was all shadowy and surreal for me. Still jet lagged, I was going through some reverse cultural shock. What if the bus did not show up, what if it's a scam. We waited and waited, and phone calls after phone calls. We were not sure if the bus was coming. Around 11 p.m., we saw a coaster, a small bus, with no passengers in it. We were asked to board. We put our luggage on the empty seats. The driver was not familiar with Islamabad, but after some struggle we reached some pizza house named Tehzeeb, where ten to fifteen passengers were picked up. Past midnight, the bus left Islamabad. The bus was a small Toyota coaster that could seat 25 people. We got the VIP treatment and were thrown in the back seats. When we complained, we were lectured by some random guy in a tone that said take it or leave it. We murmured and claimed the seats with "that's not fair." look on our faces. It was twenty-four to thirty hour bumpy, rough ride to Skardu. Now, it had become grumpy and bumpy ride. We did what we usually do in these situations, we made the best out of it. We talked, joked, and made friends. There were two classes of people travelling in this coaster, one class was well dressed, English speaking people from the city of Lahore and Karachi, and others were few Skardu's local Balti people, probably cooks, labor and porters for the team. We made good friends with Balti people, and while we were telling jokes and sharing stories, the coaster was zooming through town after town.

The driver was a charming, good looking, kid like face guy in his late teens or early twenties. Not only he knew all the shortcuts, but he also knew how to fast talk out of the check posts. Pakistan had done a decent job in stabilizing peace within her borders. But there was a price, there were check points after check points, metal detectors everywhere. These were not regular check points, these were the finger on the trigger check points. You better cooperate. Getting twenty-five passengers checked-in along with their luggage at every other check point would not be fun. The driver knew that and he would tell his story in a minute thus assuring the check post staff of no wrongdoings in the minimum possible time. We would be back on the road speeding up as if we were untouchable and unstoppable.

The driver was such a smart-ass, that at one check point he told one police officer that he was fasting and sworn on his fast he was telling the truth. Well, first of all, it was not Ramadan; second of all, it was night time. Who in the world fast during the evening? Only that driver could pull off such act and he was very smooth about it.

Since it was night travel, we did not have to deal with daytime hellish city traffic. Road was a mostly two-way highway, one lane each way. Anything that can move could be on the highway during the daytime, so we were saving time by travelling in night.

Passing Through Kaghan

In the early morning, we were in Kaghan Valley which is one of the most beautiful areas adjacent to Kashmir. It made me nostalgic; I had been here 20 years ago. I along with few friends had trekked through the entire Kaghan Valley on foot in order to go to Nanga Parbat's Fairy Meadows.

This time we were not walking through. We had different goals then and different now. A lot have changed. We were now zipping through the valley. Roads were vastly improved, but hazards were still there. At one point there were downed power lines on the road. All vehicles were stopped but only our driver dared to drive through those high voltage power lines. Power lines were few millimeters away from the coaster. Our driver almost had us electrocuted alive.

We made some pit stops, longer one in Naran, Kaghan's de-facto capital, for the breakfast. Kaghan had become more touristy now, somewhat crowded. We crossed entire Kaghan Valley by noon, which was not doable some time ago. Roads were way better, but we could have done a better job in respecting the nature. Wherever we stopped, we could easily spot trash people had left behind. And to show their best behavior people did not mind throwing out a bag full of trash through moving cars. I wished, maybe we should not have built better roads, at least not yet.

Kaghan Valley outshines the pastures and lakes of the Alps by many fold. Kaghan Valley's lake, Saif-ul-Malook, hidden and nestled under glaciated peak, Malika Parbat, is so pristine that stars come down in the night to praise its beauty. Yes, I know this because I had camped there through the night when there were only few random huts in Naran 10 miles hike away. Malika Parbat also bowed to the beauty of the lake early morning of our lone camping night.

Then there was Lulusar Lake, shaped like horse shoe, then Baser, then Gitidas village and then came the Babusar Top. I remember when we had trekked 3 days from Naran to reach Gitidas village, the entire village came out to see us out of curiosity. They probably wondered "who are these crazies." We gave their kids some medicines and candies and they gave us some bread and pure organic fresh goat milk. Today, as we passed the Gittidas village on our bus, I felt the taste of the goat milk which I hardly could take more than a sip because it was too pure for me.

Gitidas was the last village of the Kaghan valley. After crossing Gitidas our bus climbed to the Babusar Top at 13,690 ft. to cross into the Karakoram range. Babusar

Top was quiet a vista point. It's the end of Kaghan Valley and high enough to see the pastures, peaks and glaciers of the valley. We took a pit stop, savored in the vista and reboarded our bus. The bus took on the well paved and well painted road, and zigzagged into the adjacent valley of Chillas. In hours, our bus crossed Chillas town and then zigzagged further down to Karakoram Highway. We were officially in Karakoram range now.

Karakoram Highway

If something that Pakistani's are proud of in terms of construction marvel, then Karakoram Highway is the proud winner. Pakistani and Chinese literally gave blood to build Karakoram Highway. This highway starts in Abottabad, Pakistan, a town which is now internationally famous for many things now. This snaky highway then travels 810 miles all the way to Kashgar, city of Xinjiang region in China. Construction started in 1959 and it took twenty years to build the highway. 810 Pakistani's died building 501 miles of the Pakistani side highway while 200 Chinese died building Chinese section. The highway cuts through the Karakoram range and goes all the way to 15,397 feet of elevation, almost the same height of Mount Blanc, the highest peak of the Alps in Europe. It is one of the highest paved road of the world. Unofficially, it is also titled eighth wonder of the world.

Karakoram range was in sheer contrast with Kaghan Valley. Kaghan Valley was romantic while the Karakoram was wild. A wild yet mad brown Indus river cuts through the Karakoram. Indus River is the river that is responsible for birthing many civilizations in Indo-Pak subcontinent. Then the road became narrower, and drops became more straight. It was getting scarier by the hour. And when I thought it could not get any scarier than this, then it would get even more scary.

Raikot Bridge

After merging onto Karakoram Highway, which is also known as KKH, I anxiously waited for Raikot Bridge, a KKH bridge over Indus river some 50 miles before Gilgit-Baltistan's capitol city of Gilgit. Raikot Bridge was very significant to me because I had so many memories. For me, Raikot Bridge was the trailhead to Fairy Meadows of the Nanga Parbat mountain. Almost two decades ago, we had trekked through Kaghan Valley, then hitch hiked to Raikot Bridge, only to find out that we were out of food, reserves and money. We were amateurs. We then hitched a pity ride on a jingle truck all the way to Islamabad. 400 miles on a typical Pakistani cargo truck known as jingle truck broke our backs and pride.

We had showed up at Raikot Bridge the very next year after our failure. We were relatively better prepared and were a better team the second time. We again had trekked Kaghan Valley, hitched hiked to Raikot Bridge and took on the trek to Tatto village and then Fairy Meadows to our first glimpse of Nanga Parbat the merciless.

That was twenty years ago but today as our bus approached Raikot Bridge, rush of nostalgic euphoria possessed me for a moment. How could I forget all that hitch hiking and all those adventures. How could I forget that we almost slept next to scorpion's habitat at Raikot Bridge among many other misadventure.

On Skardu Road and $10 Bet

By the time I was able to calm down and relax, our

Toyota coaster made a right turn and crossed a single lane hanging bridge onto Skardu road. We had left the Karakoram highway and now we were on a single patchy road on a wilder terrain. The driver was speeding as if it was his backyard. I cringed in my seat. By this time, my feet were swollen as if I was pregnant. I checked my belly but luckily it was all flat there. I then used my pregnant feet as mercy weapon and secured better front seat next to the door.

Sitting in a single seat across the aisle was a lady in black and white *shalwar qamees*. She seemed to be by herself unlike the other woman in our bus who was accompanied by her husband. I asked her if she had done any trekking before. She told me in her British English accent mixed with some British Punjabi that she had been to Mount Everest's base camp in Nepal a year ago. I high fived her. She was a Pakistani British from Manchester, UK. She took out her iPhone and showed me a video in which she was sprinting at the Mount Everest base camp at the height of 16,000 feet or so. She then showed me her pictures of marathons and work outs regiments that she had completed or followed. She was damn fit. Her name was Bushra however based on her active life style I asked her if it was okay if I called her Bush. She didn't respond.

"I will be the one who will make it to GGLA (Gondogoro La) top first" Bush then claimed all of a sudden. I had no doubts, however, our new Balti friend Afzal, who was listening on our conversation, pitched in. His Balti blood boiled and he counter challenged Bush's challenge. He said, "I don't do workouts or run marathons, however I was born and raised in Skardu. Mountains are in my blood and I will beat anyone regardless how fit they are." This ensued claims and counter claims from both Bush and Afzal. All of this caused some excitement in the bus and the bus was divided. Half of them were rooting for Bush and half for Afzal. I brokered the deal and they settled on $10 bet for whoever reaches first.

As always, there was someone, who opposes for the sake of opposing, always. Bush was from other group and her group lead interrupted "That's not allowed." That killed all of the fun. It was the same guy who was not so friendly when we were boarding the bus in Islamabad. Somebody had forgotten their fun n chill pill. It was all business for someone. On a good note, we were able to break the ice big time and jokes were flying from all sides of the bus.

Focusing back on the road, I was seeing that at some places, half of the road had fallen thousands of feet into the river. Road was soft on edges, and our coaster would swing on one side to the river. At one point I jumped out of the bus when it was crossing a half fallen road, lunging to the river thousand feet below. I took the clue from Balti passengers; I saw them jumping out of the bus, and I followed. If they were jumping then, it must be a perilous situation. I did not want to be part of any news yet.

The landscape was scary beautiful. There was a white gold rush some time ago and people had built some stone houses on far-off cliffs and carved paths on mountains. It's hard to fathom how can one even go there let alone live there.

While we sat in our seats like frightened sheep, our driver was whistling, singing along and speeding. We were not sure why the driver was so happy, it could be the lack of sleep or tiredness, or it could be that he had nothing to lose and he wanted to take us down with him. We were in the 20th hour on-road, and the driver may have taken a nap for one hour.

Skardu, We Are Here

Luck was on our side, we made it to Skardu by the next midnight. We were stuffed in a small coaster for twenty-four hours so we couldn't feel Skardu yet but hit the bed as soon as we were shown our rooms. There will be another day, and we were relieved, sort of. We checked into Masherbrum Hotel and feasted on left over Biryani. So far I had accumulated thirty-four hours of a bus ride and twenty-four hours flight times. I was heavily jetlagged and was dodging food poisoning.

Skardu is the heart of Pakistan's Gilgit-Baltistan province. Though it sounds like Baltistan is some touristy area with fancy mountains, lakes, glaciers, flowers and fauna inhabited by color full people who play polo and dance for the pleasures of the tourists but as a matter of fact Baltistan has rich history which was peaceful and violent at times.

Baltistan, Tibet of Pakistan

Being at the western extremity of Tibet, Baltistan region was once known as Little Tibet. People of Tibetan descent who settled in this region spoke Tibetic language called Balti. The region eventually become known as Baltistan and the people became Balti people. Being from Tibetan descent majority of the people followed Buddhism one way or the other.

For centuries Baltistan was ruled by many small and independent rulers bonded with common trade interests, blood relationships, common cultural beliefs and linguistic bonding. Then came Ibrahim Shah from Kashmir and founded Maqpon dynasty in Skardu and ruled Baltistan for 700 years. Kashmir is another paradise like region of Himalayan belt next to Karakoram, with relatively easy access from Northern India. By Sixteenth century Muslim Sufi missionaries from Kashmir eventually inspired majority of Balti people to convert to Noorbakshia's Sufi Islam. After certain events and incidents Shiite Islam became more popular. Before falling to Dogras, the Maqpon dynasty extended rule Gilgit and Ladakh regions in addition to Baltistan.

Then came the Dogras of Kashmir in Ninteenth century and controlled Baltistan. Dogras acceded to India at the time of India Pakistan partition in 1947. People of Baltistan revolted and as a result some part of Baltistan and Ladakh became part of Pakistan. Kashmir got split between India and Pakistan. Kashmir split became a lifelong territorial dispute and a cause of multiple wars between the neighboring India and Pakistan. Pakistan in 2009 declared Baltistan and neighboring Gilgit area as an autonomous province and called it Gilgit-Baltistan province. Gilgit-Balistan also known as GB has given Balti people new form of proud identity and some autonomy.

Our Team

It took me some time to figure out who was with whom. We were sharing bus and jeeps with different teams and for me it was getting frustrating. I didn't want someone to tell me whom to talk to whom not to talk to. Yes this had actually happened. The lead of one of the group actually barged into our room in Masherbrum Hotel to tell us that we shouldn't be talking to their team members. I promptly turned him away and complained to our tour operator. It turned out there were two teams that were being managed by common set of guides, cooks and porters provided by the single tour operator. We were in the team who contracted directly with the tour operator. Other people were in a sub team of a person who contracted with the same tour operator as ours.

My team members were Ahtisham, Salman, Nauman Siddique, Nouman Khan, Saad, Kashif, Asim, and me. Yes, we had two Nauman's. Ahtisham, nicknamed Shami, was a mechanical engineer at Engro Fertilizer, Dhorki, Sindh. Salman, nicknamed Sallu, was an entrepreneur from Lahore, and he was running a perfume business out of Shalmi market in old Lahore. Nauman S. was a metallurgy engineer and was a dedicated assistant professor at University of the Punjab, Lahore. The other Nouman, Nouman Khan, was from Lahore also. He was a manager in the TDCP, Tourism Development Corporation of Pakistan, and was on an official trip to reconnaissance the Concordia Trek for the possibility of offering Concordia Trek as a package to the adventure seeking tourists. Along with his full-time job, Nouman K. was pursuing his Ph.D. in marketing from the University of the Punjab, Lahore. Asim was a seasoned IT professional and was working as an IT manager at a telco company in Islamabad. Kashif, my old time friend, was a real estate guru in Multan. Saad was in his final years of engineering from NUST (National University of Science and Technology), Islamabad. Saad was into soccer and traveling.

Side Trip to Deosai, the Land of Giants

While in Skardu, my body was learning to respond to

new weather and water, yet Asim wanted to see Deosai plains. It would be a minimum ten hours jeep trip if we rushed. Rest was very much needed, but I was easily convinced. All I had to do was sit in the jeep, right? As a bribe, I was given the privilege of the front seat.

Two other folks had agreed to go with us, but they were asked to bail out by their team lead. It was a team thing that they were protective about, and probably they were branding their adventure company. We didn't care what was their team up to and we went with our plans. Our Balti friend from the bus, Pyare Afzal, arranged for the jeep for us at the cost of Rs 10,000 (100 USD). He was a Skardu resident and had been in Nigeria for work for a long time. He was in Pakistan to see his family for a short period but was forced to extend his stay due to some delay in his Nigerian visa processing. His actual name was Wazir Afzal. "Pyare Afzal" was the popular television drama in Pakistan just a year ago, by the way. Afzal informed us that Shami would like to tag along for Deosai. Shami was a cool kid, intelligent and witty. We hit right off when we were introduced. For Shami, this was the first time to Concordia trek. He had hiked to Nanga Parbat Basecamp last year and got hooked.

We left Skardu 7 a.m. in a rented Toyota Cruiser. Salamat was our driver. We had Pyare Afzal with us. Skardu was quiet mystical in the morning. Stone walled houses with tall trees, wide streets and the aroma in the air made Skardu very romantic. However, our rented Toyota Land Cruiser jeep was not in a mood for any romance at all. The tire punctured every hour or so forcing us to take breaks. This added to our anxiety and brought lots of what if's in our head.

We stopped at Sadpara dam of the Sadpara village and we couldn't help but notice kids playing cricket near stream down below. There were wide white soft sand and gravel patches which made a good cricket pitch and ground. We then breezed through small farms of cauliflower, potatoes, etc. Apricots and mulberries were the locally grown delicious fruit. Khanda and Zaan are sweet dishes made of these fruits. These delicious dishes are never sold outside as they are home meals and consumed at home exclusively. That Sunday we covered Deosai plains on the jeep. Deosai was mesmerizing beautiful. Deosai was a vast giant green meadow plains at the average height of 13,497 feet. All the jeep ride was on dirt stone trail crisscrossing through lush meadows. We stopped at vista points such as Chota Pani, Bara Pani, Sheosar Lake, and Sadpara dam.

Gold Digging Ants

Around 540 B.C., Herodotus, a Greek philosopher, had mentioned Deosai in his book. He mentioned in one of his famous history books that there was region in far east Persian India in which there lived large size gold digging ants. These ants dig gold in their burrows and people then collect the gold dust and would live off that. Because of the gold dust these ants were of golden color. These gold digging ants were actually the Golden Marmots of Deosai and it is believed that Herodotus misinterpreted the Persian translation of the word Marmots in Persian.

For me, the highlight was to see a small colony of the wild Golden Marmots, I mean the gold digging ants. Five of them were huddled together while two of them at guard. I guess they were taking break from their gold digging activities. They sure looked like that they were sprayed with golden dust. Wild Golden Marmots were all so cute. Shami attempted to take pictures and once he closed in, Marmots disappeared underground as if they never existed.

There was a reason Asim insisted on visiting Deosai plains. Deosai is one of the highest plateaus on earth. Deosai has an average elevation of 13,497 ft. and covers 1200 square miles of protected area. These plains are only second to Chang Thang Plateau in Tibet. Deosai plains are home to endangered Himalayan Brown Bear, golden marmot, Himalayan Ibex, gray wolf, snow leopards and red foxes. A unique variety of birds ranging from peregrine falcons to golden eagles, vultures, and many other birds call this place home. Given its unique geological location, flower, fauna, and butterflies are one of a kind in these wild plains.

Deosai had always been on my wish list, but I did not want to risk the K2 Concordia trek for Deosai. I feared that I would get exhausted to death before I could even start. However, I was glad that I was able to visit albeit, only for few hours. Deosai was after all Deosai.

Back to Islamabad, Probably?

Back in Skardu, the gang went out to scavenge last minute items from Skardu Bazaars(markets). In the evening, Skardu was very much alive, it was hustling and bustling with people. While I rested at the hotel, the gang was able to secure some name brand items at very reasonable prices, though items were slightly used. Foreign expeditions sometimes leaves items behind for Skardu merchants to sell at Skardu markets. You could score a Merrill shoe for $10 that usually costs $150, used though.

Back in the hotel, that night, my fear of getting sick beyond recovery came to some reality. I couldn't sleep all night, and felt I was all choked. I was sleepless, breathless, and my body was too fatigued even to close my eyes. In nervousness I took pain killers, antibiotic pills, and high altitude medicine and that made things worse. In few hours we were to load ourselves in the jeeps that would get us to starting point of K2 Concordia. It wouldn't be happening for me it seemed like.

In the early morning, I informed Kashif and Asim that I was too sick to make it to Concordia and I would be more of a liability then a partner and they should continue without me. They both said that they would abandon their plans as well, I would be flattered but I wanted to be prudent as money was already paid and terms clearly state no refunds. I started packing my bags. Asim suggested that we should talk to Pyare Afzal and seek advice. Afzal brought Ishaq, our tour operator, with him and after some considerations, they suggested that I should at least try to make it to Askole and then I can rest up there while the team could go per schedule. When and if I got better, I should be able to catch up with the team on next stages of the trek.

Asim and Kashif then went out to spend time with other team members and check out our departure affairs. I was in my room curled up on the bed. I didn't know what was happening. Was it food poisoning, water bacteria, high altitude, exhaustion or something else. I didn't know. I crawled to the bathroom and sat next to commode hoping that somehow throwing up might help, provided if I could throw up ever. I thought all the scenarios and thought about how much trouble I went through to come this far, and now I would have to return before I could start. I was not even sure what had happened to me. A sudden rush of emotions overcame me, and I broke down, and sobbed. I cried like a child, alone in that bathroom next to a commode, thousands of miles away from home. I didn't know after how long, I finally threw up. It was not pleasant, but my body that was all clogged started to open up. It was food poisoning. I had food poisoning before but I never had it that bad. That disgusting, ugly vomit gave me hope. I hoped to recover, and I was relieved.

I gathered my will power and packed my bags for Askole but not for Islamabad.

Figure 4: Top: Babusar Top overlooking Kaghan Valley; Bottom left: Naran of Kaghan bustling, which was only few huts, not so long ago; Bottom right: Babusar Top vista point

Figure 5: Top Left: Karakorum Highway landslide area near Chilas; Top right: Our guide, Afzal, inspecting a damaged fellow coaster on Skardu Road; Bottom: Skardu signature resort (photo by Salman Zakir)

Figure 6: Top left: Golden Marmots, the gold diggers, of Deosai (photo by Shami); Top right: An abandoned bridge in Deosai, Bara Pani, which had always fascinated me; Bottom left: Sheosar Lake, 13,589 ft., Deosai (photo by Shami); Bottom right: Deosai plains from west entrance (photo by Shami)

4

SKARDU TO ASKOLE

It was Monday morning, our scheduled departure time was 7 a.m., but we did not leave Skardu until 10 a.m. Desi standard time management at its best. Desi is a term used to address ethnicities from Indo-Pak subcontinent who are also known as brown people to some. Our destination was Askole village. Askole was the last town reachable by jeep track. After that we would be on foot for weeks.

There was a festive mode in the Masherbrum hotel lobby and porch. Five jeeps were parked in hotel porch for our luggage and us. I overheard that there was a roadblock at half way and we would need to change jeeps at the blockage. It was cloudy that day. I prayed for the sun and unobstructed views. Fingers crossed.

Once we left Skardu, we continued East along the river Indus on a paved road for half an hour or so and then took a left turn toward Shigar Valley. We took on a long single lane hanging bridge and span made of wooden planks suspended by wires supported by foundations on each side of the river. We crossed the merciless Indus river and entered a white sand desert.

Our single road was cutting through white sand dunes and disappearing into the mountains ahead of us. White sand desert among those brown mountains was quite a unique landscape, and Shami shouted in excitement, "Stop the jeep, stop the jeep. This place is just like in the movies". The driver hit the brakes, and we stopped at white sand desert for a photo session. We posed for some funny pictures, and the few of us laid down in the middle of the road for some clicks for a child in us.

Back on the road we then entered Shigar valley and then Shigar town which was decent size town with small settlements spread around wheat fields and apricot gardens. There was even a crossing in a town which was guarded by the traffic sergeant. It was funny to see a traffic warden in a clean white uniform diligently controlling the traffic which was nothing more than a few kids running around, may be a motorbike or so and random jeep like ours. We stopped in the middle of the crossing and chatted a bit with the traffic sergeant and went our way.

Shigar town had historical significance and to tell about it there was a fort and a museum. Shigar Fort was worth visiting but we had bigger plans so we conveniently skipped. After few miles, our jeep stopped in the middle of an apricot garden. A short Balti guy from other jeep brought some apricots. The small yellowish squishy apricots were full of distinct taste. A taste that fades away from these apricots as soon as these apricots leave this Shigar Valley. You got to be in the Shigar Valley to enjoy these apricots. That short guy was Munna Ibrahim. More on him later.

By afternoon we had left Shigar Valley way behind. No

more paved road after Shigar town. It was all dirt track which allowed only jeeps to travel. Jeep trailed up through mountains with drops to the mad Indus River. It was an amazing experience watching the river going through the desert. One can see big dark brown mountains with numerous waterfalls every couple of hundreds of yards or so. There must be a good supply of glaciers behind these mountains somewhere. One could see two rivers merging. Braldu Nala (Nala means stream in Urdu language) was joining the mighty Indus River, making Indus River more potent.

Now, we were with Braldu Nala. We had left Indus behind. Sometimes we were too close to the river and sometimes we passed through open wheat crops fields, apricot gardens. Sometimes we would pass through rocks only sections and sometimes through long stretches of flowing mud. The jeep ride was pretty bouncy. I was hurting bad, and I was having severe headache. My bandana was helping. I couldn't wait to dump the Jeep and feel the fresh air. Too much diesel smoke was surrounding our jeeps. Only our jeeps were polluting otherwise it was all fresh, clean air. The jeeps were crawling at such a slow speed that one can smell the diesel of one's jeep. Jeep was moving slower than the diesel it was fuming out.

Fallen Jeep Track

Around 1 p.m., we reached the roadblock area. The road, which was nothing but a dirt track, had fallen into the river. Only enough track was left for one person to walk through. We walked to the other side to claim our rides on the jeeps waiting on other sides. Rs 100 was given to porters to carry a bag. It took us one hour to be back on the road again. Around 2 p.m., we were at Dassu checkpoint. It's an army checkpoint. Our identity cards were checked, and army staff diligently jotted down our emergency contact information and other essential information. Passports and permits of the foreigners were checked. My NICOP (National Identity Card for Overseas Pakistani) was welcomed there. A jeep full of porters was also required to register.

It took 40 minutes at the checkpoint. After Dassu checkpoint we took a hanging bridge to cross Braldu Nala and now Braldu Nala was on our right side. We then passed a charming tiny village, Bali. We then crossed the hanging bridge one more time. Now, Nala was on the left. We would play this game of crossing rivers many times over the next four hours.

Around 3:30 p.m., we passed through Apo Ali Gon village. We stopped there for lunch. At 8,483 feet we couldn't wait for our *daal roti* (lentils with bread) and chicken curry. We feasted on *daal roti* with Braldu Nala flowing close by. Our jeep was low on air pressure. Driver took out a bicycle pump and used the bicycle pump to pump air into the jeep's tires. I was amused by this. It was totally minimalistic approach. By the way being minimalist was getting fashionable in Silicon Valley these days.

Back on the dirt track, we crossed Pakora village by 6 p.m. The jeep track was narrower and steeper, and we were navigating through sharp switchbacks. In no time we passed the Hotu Village and then Hotu hanging bridge. Now, Braldu Nala was on our right side.

Around 6:20 p.m., we saw a green patch in the far distance and thought it was Askole, but it turned out to be Thomal Village. We were then able to see Thomal Peak, our first peak so far. We entered Thomal Village and saw kids playing cricket. It was unbelievable. Is this a cricket country or what? At 9,644 feet high, in a remote village in a remote area, cricket was being played with passion.

At 7 p.m., we reached the Askole. Askole, the last village in the Karakorum and our trail head for the K2 Base Camp was way more unique than I had imagined. For an outsider, Askole was a one-lane community, few small shops selling basic amenities could be seen on sides. At the end of that single lane, there was a small, two-story, red-bricked, six room hotel building. We were to camp out in that hotel yard. There were few restrooms in the hotel's yard, and they were in sheer contrast to the beauty of Askole.

Sun was setting and before it would become pitch dark, I ventured out for a lone stroll in this lone village. Askole though not much populated was full of life. All I heard were laughter of people around me. Playful youth gave me smiles and they all looked content and happy. It all looked like a well-connected, well content, and very cheerful community nestled in the remote part of the remote world. I was instantly jealous of their contentment. I work so hard in the pursuit of happiness and here it was so obvious simple and right in front of me. Askole was a magical oasis in the wild desert of Karakoram.

Our dying cell phone signals were completely dead on our first camping night, and we already began tasting remoteness. I skipped the meal, and in next fifteen minutes, I was in my sleeping bag. I desperately needed good sleep. The tent was little tight for three people with our bags, but it felt like five stars to me. I needed to recover, and I wasted no time in falling asleep.

Figure 7: Top left: Fallen jeep track near Dassu Checkpost before Askole (photo by Salman Zakir); Top right: Dassu Checkpost jeep exchange (photo by Salman Zakir); Bottom: Shigar Valley as seen from Skardu-Askole jeep track; (photos by Nouman K.)

Figure 8: Top left: Skardu-Askole road (photo by Nouman K.); Top right: A Balti boy offering fresh apricots to the guest, Shigar Valley. Bottom left: Skardu-Askole road (photo by Salman Zakir); Bottom right: Getting jeeps ready at Hotel Mashabrum, Skardu (photo by Nouman K.)

5

DAY 1, ASKOLE TO JHOLA

Askole was a happy town. There were fields, gardens, rivers, waterfalls, tall trees, open meadows, all surrounded by peaks with unique texture and demeanor that made Askole looked more naturally beautiful than its counterpart remote towns in the modern developed world. It was too bad that we were in Askole for one night only. Staying in Askole for few days would had been quiet an adventure and would had been very therapeutic. But we had to let Askole go for pursuit of the K2.

Twenty Eggs Debacle

Who could guess that twenty eggs could have almost wrapped up the trip? The *shehri babus* (the city boys), had a certain confidence in the way they carried themselves. They would assume that things would be taken care as long as they had money in their pockets. They acted like they owned the world. Well, things were little different there especially starting from Askole, the last settlement on this part of the world. Food needed to be carried on foot or on mules from then onward.

No replenishment was possible for next fifteen days. The *shehri babu* group from Lahore and Karachi went crazy over the breakfast and consumed more eggs than our team cook had envisioned. In cities, it doesn't mean anything, but here it escalated quickly. Cook argued if that's the way food was going to be consumed then the entire group would be starving in the middle of nowhere. Out of desperation, the cook submitted his resignation in protest. Somehow, the situation was mediated upon assurances on some random guys.

Just to clarify, our mess tent was separate from the other group, so we were unaware of the twenty egg issue. I became aware of this at Korofong, the next stop, when I sat with the cooks and porters for some chit chat.

First Day of Trekking

It was Tuesday, and it would be our first day of trekking. We were officially embarking on the trek which was supposed to be the journey of our lifetime. I woke up little early at 5 a.m. I was feeling better and had an inclination that I would be able to pull it off and was determined. By 6 a.m., I was in our mess tent with my team. We were officially separated from the other team whom we were told not to get in touch with.

After breakfast of a simple omelet with white flour *roti paratha* (thin wheat flat dough sautéed in oil) and some jam and butter, we packed our bags. Our bags were then weighed and assigned to porters. We were allowed 12.5 kilos per person. For me it was a luxury. A large number of onlookers and potential porters invaded the campsite. It was a festival-like atmosphere. There was only one trek that goes out of Askole, and we were told to start walking that trek.

Around 7 a.m., we started our trek with our daypacks stuffed with day clothing, snacks, camera, sunscreen, emergency medical kit, and water. After half an hour of pleasant hike, the valley started opening up, and we could see green field patches across the Baltoro river on our right side. On our left side, it was all brown mountains with waterfalls after every thirty minutes or so. The trail was decently wide. A Honda CG125 motorbike crossed us. There were still signs of town like life. A CG 125 is a 125cc motorcycle and is very popular in Pakistan. And these motorbikes were now making their way to such remote areas.

At one point on the trail, I ran into a stray mule coming from the opposite side. Interestingly, the mule stepped aside to let me through. The mule turned around and kept its eyes on me as I passed through. Once I was at a reasonable distance, it strutted away. I challenge you to try experiencing this kind of hospitality at any seven star resort.

After one hour of trekking, around 8 a.m., we entered the CKNP (Central Karakorum National Park) entry post. A bright, handsome guy with a long face and long hair welcomed us. His name was Ishaq, and he collected Rs 850 entry fee per person. There were different tariff for different type of activities. For foreigners entry fees were $30 and above. I didn't think that was that bad.

Around 9 a.m., I crossed the hanging pedestrian bridge over the Braldu Nala. It was literally swinging and made my head spin as I crossed. The Braldu Nala was on my left side from then on. Before this bridge, there were steep and sharp switchbacks with drops to Braldu Nala. The trail at such points was narrow enough for only one person to pass through. After the bridge, the valley was broad and the trek turned into a sand pebble path.

Everybody had their own hiking style. Some walked fast, some slow, some packed light, some packed everything other than kitchen sink and some just dragged themselves cursing. I always started slow, for me important was to get into groove, to get my body set in motion and take in the surroundings. First hour was always the best as the body would be fresh and there was plenty of energy and fresh morning breeze made it very pleasant. At the start, I was one of the slowest, I didn't knew how many miles I had to hike that day, I didn't know the terrain but I did know that it would be entire day of hiking. So I took time for my hiking engine to warm up and let the majority had a head start.

Once I warmed up, I started to catch up with other hikers. I caught up with a husband wife hiker couple with whom I had shared bus ride from Islamabad to Skardu. They were exhausted to death; at any moment they would fall to ground and eat the dust. They were little overweight and were struggling with each step. I was told by their team lead to not to talk to any of his team members. However, I couldn't see the couple suffer. I asked the couple if I could help them if they don't mind. They were good sports. I inspected their back packs which were dangling low to the ground. I adjusted their back pack belts. Brought their back backs at or higher to their hips. The lady was wearing scarf and was dressed heavy. I asked her to take extra jackets off. After some adjustments, I saw signs of relief on their faces. They were carrying lot of stuff in their back packs. I told them unless they had done backpacking before with such weight, they would be better off giving their extra weight to the porters. They were from Karachi and the lady was a professional photographer. She was carrying all the lenses and accessories in her day back pack.

I then caught up with Bush. She had a good pace and she had started way earlier than me. I was surprised, how come I was able to catch up to her. After some pleasantries I asked her how did she compare this trek with Mount Everest trek or was it too early to comment. She said "Mt. Everest trek is not even close to this trek." She paused then said "This." She paused again, caught some breath and said "This is so wild and so remote!" She then stopped for a water break and I continued my march. Ah, that's how I was able to catch up. She was taking water breaks. I had water bladder in my back pack and I was sipping water without taking water breaks, which gave me an advantage. To her credit she was also waiting up for the hikers whom she had teamed up with.

Korofong

At the seven mile mark, around 10 a.m., I entered the Korofong site. Kashif and Nouaman K. welcomed me with warm smiles. Each site or a stop was also called a stage there. At 10,147 feet, Korofong site was nothing but a cluster of trees with running semi-clean water. Fong means stone in Balti language and Koro means round. There was supposed to be a one big round stone somewhere, but all stones looked round to me.

I saw some local folks huddled together. I saw an opening and sat next to them. They were welcoming and turned out to be our group porters, cook, and guides. They were very cool guys. I could clearly notice they were sunburned and everyone had on old shoes, and they had many holes in their socks. This job did not make them wealthy, and I could clearly tell that they were hardly getting their ends meet. One of the guides gave us the inside scoop that an Askole porter, as a tradition, had to make love to his wife and take a mandatory shower before embarking on such journey. Mostly women work on fields, and their husbands had to track them down causing delays in teams logistics. Upon the porter's return, they were supposed to take a shower and then make love to their wives. There were interesting theories around this, and I would not go into that much details.

Around noon, we were finally done with Maggie noodle soup, some biscuits, and green tea. We left for Jhola, our next stage where we were to camp for the night.

After trekking of rough five more miles in light rain and wind, we reached Jhola camp at 3 p.m. A mile before the Jhola camp, we crossed a hanging wooden pedestrian bridge called Jhola. Before the bridge was made, there used to be a zip line with a trolley (Jhola means trolley in Urdu language) clipped to the zip line. Trekkers were to sit in the Jhola and were pushed across the wild river. That bridge made my head spin. Rapids were so furious. I could only imagine what it would have been like if I were to cross this on the Jhola zip line. The rain that I was cursing while trekking was, in fact, a blessing. There was no shade at all and the direct sun heat could have increased chances of heat stroke significantly. As a matter of fact, the first two days of Concordia Trek are the hottest and chances of getting heat strokes are higher.

Jhola

Jhola campsite elevation was 10,300 feet. The campsite was easily spot able from far. On arriving the Jhola campsite, one can easily spot tiny house like gray structures erected on slopes. These structures were the toilets built on top of dug holes. Water was supplied through pipes in the common area, where you would fill your *lota* (a plastic water vessel), bucket or bottle for your cleaning needs. Some toilets have English style commode, and some have local style, known as an Indian commode, on which one need to squat.

Kashif was 25 minutes early, and Asim was 45 minutes behind. Our guide put us in a stone-bricked walled shelter while our tents were being set up. The Shingha Nala peak could be seen from there. As teams started arriving, the site became little crowded.

Jhola was also a junction point where teams going to Snow Lake split. We will not be seeing many Snow Lake trekkers whom we had befriended on this journey. The Snow Lake was also a popular destination for adventure seeker. The Snow Lake trek was more challenging then Concordia. There was no K2 there, so there was no charm for me. I heard really good things about the Snow Lake trek though. Snow Lake, which is not a lake, is a glacial basin at the height of 16,000 feet in the northern tip of Karakoram range. It would be easily at least seven days of trekking to the Snow Lake from where we were.

At 5 p.m., we had green tea with biscuits, and then we huddled in kitchen tent. Here we were introduced to our top guide, Munna Ibrahim. A know it all guy with a permanent smile and bright lit eyes and unlimited supply of energy, Munna Ibrahim was charming funny, and his wits made him our best friend and an ally for the entire trip. We had lots of gup-shup (chit chat) with Munna Ibrahim, our team teased him a lot, and eventually he named our group ballsy group. I will let you do the translation. Ibrahim Munna was the lead guy and a seasoned guide with twenty-five years of experience. He was of Balti descent and was from Hushe village. Most of all he was very smart and funny and a gem of a person. We all loved him as soon as he opened his loud mouth. After 7 p.m., we had dinner and went to our tents, we were dead tired and slept like babies.

Figure 9: Top left: Trail leading to CKNP entry post (photo by Nouman K.); Top right: Munna at Askole Campsite watching our bags before handing over to the porters (photo by Nouman K.); Bottom: Pedestrian hanging bridge on Askole-Korofong trail (photo by Salman Zakir)

Figure 10: Top Left: Askole-Jhola trail along Braldu Nala; Right: A narrow and steep stretch of Askole-Jhola trail (photo by Salman Zakir); Bottom left: The wheat fields of Askole Village

Figure 11: Top Left: Bhullah Peak, 6,294 meters (20,650 ft.), as seen from the Jhola Campsite (photo by Salman Zakir); Top right: A selfie with cooks and guides at Korofong Stage; Bottom: Jhola Campsite in late afternoon (photo by Salman Zakir)

6

DAY 2, JHOLA TO PAIYU

I was not a morning person and I was surprised how fresh I felt when on Wednesday, July 20th 2016, I woke up 4:30 a.m. comfortably and without much struggle. I could hear birds whistling and horses and mules neighing and snorting. I could listen to a constant rhythmic sound of Braldu Nala in the background. We had a long trek ahead of us that day.

Kashif woke up with an excruciating pain in his legs and groin area. It got us worried. For his first day of trekking, he wore jeans, leggings and put waterproof trousers on top of it. Three layers of thick fabric pants and eleven miles of strenuous trekking had almost crippled him. I had strongly advised him not to wear jeans, but he needed to learn it on his own, and he did, I think. He took some painkillers to ease the pain. We joked and declared him a cry baby. He was not happy with our jokes.

We had breakfast in the mess tent at 6 a.m.: omelet and white *roti paratha* with sides of honey, jam, etc. We then packed our bags and handed them to the porters. I was feeling spoiled. Meals were prepared for us, bags were carried by porters, tents were pitched, packed and unpacked by porters. I had never backpacked like this before. I felt guilty but I let the things took it course. Some people made living on this.

Around 06:35 a.m., all of our team member huddled; Kashif became our lead *maulvi* (an imam) and prayed for the safe and blessed journey. It is customary in Pakistan to say Islamic prayers before embarking on any kind of travel. "*Subhanallazi saqqara lana haza wama kunna, lahoo muqrineen, wa inna ila rabbina la munqaliboon.*". Which translates to "Praise be to Allah Glory unto to Him who has subjected this (transportation) for us, though we were unable to subdue it. Behold we are assuredly to return unto our Lord."

Soon we were on the trail to our next stage, Burdumal. There were couple of steep gains on an otherwise rocky sand path with the river on the right side down below. The trek was mostly wide but not that flat. I could see some snowy peaks in the distance. Overall, it was very broad valley giving me the impression of open area with plain brown mountains at both sides without any new formation. In three hours, we completed the first stage of the day. No hanging bridges today. It turned out to be 7.5 miles since we started this morning.

This was second day of trekking and so far I was not that impressed. It was beautiful, wild, remote and it had a cultural touch but was it worth coming all the way from San Francisco? I wondered. To ease on the boredom, I would say hi to every porter and chat with them. They would always respond with smiling face. For them it was another work day. They were taking cigarette's breaks under random rocks. Something like water cooler meetings of white color workers of the corporate world of the U.S. Porters were listening to the music on their Nokia 3200 phones. Some had beads in their hands and were constantly praying.

I was close to the Burdumal stage when I heard a popular Indian song "O Mehbooba, Mehbooba" being a played on a passing by youthful porter's Nokia 3200 mobile phone. Mehbooba means sweetheart in Urdu language. I teased the porter, "So where is your Mehbooba, still searching?". He sheepishly said "Not possible in these mountains." and then disappeared. Though in good mood, he didn't want to deal with smart ass conversation with me at that time. For few minutes, I heard echoes of "O Mehbooba, Mein Dooba." Oh sweetheart, I am drowning. Save me.

Burdumal Stage and the Injured Porter

The Burdumal campsite, at 10,500 feet, had four adjacent huts used mainly as seasonal canteen and storage. The seasonal canteen was minimally stocked with amenities such as cigarettes and biscuits etc. A small flat area was sectioned using stones, and these stones would mark the boundaries for campsites. At some distance but close to the trek, there were waist-high stone-walled pairs of toilets with pits in the center with no running water close by.

It was bright and sunny, and there was no shade, I took this opportunity to test out my solar panel. Because there was no shade and lack of pleasant views, we were not that impressed by this site. I believed the temperature was seventy-five Fahrenheit to eighty Fahrenheit with no humidity. One liter of Pepsi was on sale for Rs 500 (5 USD), which was usually Rs. 50 (.50 USD) back in plains. We were content with cold water from a nearby stream. Kashif and Nouman were early. Asim reached late and was really exhausted. Kudos to Kashif that even after this setback he would be the first one to reach the next stage.

While we were resting, we were approached by our group's lead porter, Wali, and he asked if we could help one of his injured porters. We were not sure but seeing we probably were their only hope we agreed to take a look. I don't recall porter's name, but we were somewhat stunned when he showed his burn injury on his left side bum. It must be four inches in diameter burn injury with the skin peeled off exposing red flesh. He was carrying a stove which was so hot that it severely burned part of his left hip. My guess was that it was at least a first degree burn.

Luckily in my carry-on medical kit, I had specialized burn wound bandages. Nouman K. stepped forward and volunteered to help. I provided the alcohol wipes and cut the burn dressing from the medical kit. We told the porter that we would be cleaning his wound with wipes and it would sting. The porter lit a cigarette and took deep puffs while Nouman cleaned his wound and peeled off the loose skin. We then bandaged his wound and advised him not to do strenuous physical activity until the wound would heal. He gave us weird look when we told him not to carry any weight. He thanked us nonetheless. He could not afford not to carry his assigned load. He would be carrying the weight that was 25 kilos, all the way, and back. After all, he had a family to support. We gave him some painkillers and asked him to come to us for a follow-up.

Though we were proud to help the poor porter, it made me wonder about porter's life and the hazards in their profession they face every day. Do they always have to rely on people like us? I thought they deserved better than this.

We were not to camp at the Burdumal, but we were supposed to wait up for rest of the team. Once a few folks caught up, we then had the highly anticipated soup which was nothing but Maggie Noodles. Maggie Noodles were packaged noodles like Ramen noodles, which are widely popular in the US. We then had green tea and biscuits. We craved for a real lunch but were happy with Maggie Noodles, biscuits, green tea and some dry fruits. Something was everything in this wilderness. We were then on our way to Paiyu campsite after spending two to three hours at this site.

Burdumal - Paiyu - Mule Train and the Scary Landslide

At the Burdumal, after we refilled our water bottles and water bladders, around noon we left for Paiyu. The terrain was similar but this time river was close but way down. The trail was narrow and was tilted towards drops with loose sand and gravel. Also, the trail had long steep climbs on wet stones. Drops were deep and would scare you for your life. The mules on the trail caused another problem. They walked in a line and at some places they would be slow and at other places they would pick the pace. There were situations, where I was behind the mules eating their dust, then between the mules and then slightly ahead of mules. To avoid the mule train, I would hike quickly to cross them and would get exhausted then I would find the mules on my behind again soon enough.

Then there was an active landslide area where rocks were falling every half an hour or so. One of the porters told us to cross as fast as possible. There was no trail, so I ran, jumped, and hopped the stones while avoiding fall into the river. It was exhausting, but I kept leaping the rocks one at a time. I pictured myself having hit by rock traveling at bullet speed, and it scared me. After this landslide area, the valley widened up again, and I could see the Baltoro river splitting into multiple branches and merging into one and then splitting again. The Baltoro river spread was an unusual and a refreshing sight. The trail was somewhat easier, but the slopes were still there.

At Paiyu

Around 2:30 p.m., I entered Paiyu. First I saw the similar cluster of Italian toilets as in Jhola. As a first impression, the Paiyu campsite looked more like a stable of mules rather than a campsite. Surprisingly, the campsite provided great shade because of a vast number of trees. It was the first shade of the day, and it was a relief. The campsite was on slopes and had layered flat areas of four to five floors if you will. There was running water, but it was little muddy. We were not sure how stream water was used by the party of mules and people above us. The Paiyu was at 11,155 ft. and was approximately 5.5 miles from the Korofong stage.

That day we had trekked thirteen miles with no shade on a wet, steep trail and we were exhausted. As usual Kashif and

Nouman K. were early and then I, and then Asim and others would come late exhausted. There was no shade on the trail, and I noticed many trekkers with dry lips, sure sign of dehydration. It was not fun getting dehydrated on such long trek and one could easily lose focus then misstep or fall. Carrying extra water was always helpful.

I noticed weird large flies at the Paiyu campsite, and I cursed myself for not carrying bug spray. The views of the river were incredible, and today we were able to see the stones covered Baltoro glacier. The next day was a mandatory rest day. Most of our team members had blisters on their feet, and they were hurting badly. I gave them my blister treating moleskin and advised them not do anything funny with blisters and let the blister heal itself.

Nouman K. had fallen into a side stream while crossing it. We shared notes on how to avoid foot injuries. Nouman K. suggested using Talcum Powder, a popular baby powder made from cosmetic talc, on socks to prevent moisture and blisters. I suggested wearing two pairs of socks. One as an inner liner and one outer woolen pair. Both must be non-cotton and both must be moisture wicking. So far it was working magic for me. I suggested the same to the others. We discussed and shared helpful tips. I also shared my geeky tips. After seeing moleskin doing magic on their blisters, they were sold on any idea that I would throw at them. My suggestions were finally being welcomed.

Around 7 p.m., we were given dinner, rice, etc. We crashed in our tents soon after. Next day was a rest day, and our plans were to try to regain our strength.

Figure 12: Top left: Drops to Braldu Nala at Jhola-Paiyu trail; Top right: Trekkers navigating Jhola-Paiyu trail; Bottom: Burdumal Stage (photo by Nouman K.)

Figure 13: All: Porters taking break and/or in action on Jhola-Paiyu trail
(Photos: Top left by Nouman K.; Top right & bottom by Salman Zakir)

Figure 14: Left: Sharing trail with the mules (photo by Salman Zakir); Top right: A stretch of narrow Jhola-Paiyu trail with steep drops. Bottom Right: The Jhola hanging bridge (photo by Nouman K.)

7

DAY 3, PAIYU REST DAY AND SIDE ADVENTURE

It was the third day of trekking, and we were hit with a rest day. I thought it was too early for rest but eventually, I realized it was a wise thing to do. The Concordia trek and its stages were well planned and adopted. There were multiple factors in play, including altitude and complexity of the current terrain and the challenge upcoming trail. Our guide, Munna Ibrahim, had told us that he had seen many porters and mules falling into Braldu Nala never to be seen again. The Paiyu rest day was to recover the nerves of the porters and celebrate the twenty-eight miles into the remoteness.

As a custom, the porters on this rest day sacrifice a goat and feast on it. This goat was a thank you gift to the porters on behalf of the teams which had hired them. We chipped in Rs. 600 (6 USD) each. The porters were to sacrifice the goat in the afternoon and feast in the night. There were none of the usual dancing or singing festivities as it was a mourning month for the Balti porters.

It was a lazy morning for us. We decided to wash our clothes and ourselves. Luckily, we found washing detergent powder brand name Brite for Rs. 50 (.50 USD) from the canteen. We then grabbed a bucket nearby water tank and soaked clothes in it. Asim was determined that he would wash the clothes and nobody objected. We happily let Asim wash the clothes, and we grabbed another bucket and a small plastic pan for our shower. We filled the bucket with water and used a plastic pan to shower. We used one of the clean toilets as shower rooms. It was sunny and the water was glacier cold, but we held our breath and poured the water on us. This rest day was the day we had enough time to talk to each other and know each other.

One Polish trekker, Andrew, from a small Polish team decided to summit a close by peak. He went to the mountain top with intensity and spirit but came back with an injured hand. We found out that he had slipped bad and he had used his hands to grab whatever he could to stop his fall. He bruised his hands badly but saved himself from a dangerous fall. Summits, even small could threaten ones existence. Andrew's wife Viola, who had decided to stay back, bandaged her husband's wounds outside their tent. She had a concerned and content look on her face. Concerned that her husband was injured and content that it was not that serious. It was a gentle reminder, though.

Once we were done with our domestic chores, Nouman K., Asim, and I decided to climb the nearby mountain to look for the Trango Towers. We wanted to climb high enough to take a glimpse of the Trango Towers. There was no trail per se. We went high enough and took a break on a big isolated rock. I shared some tips on rock climbing just for fun. We had a couple of close calls and we did manage to get a glimpse of what we thought were the Trango Towers. We were back by afternoon. Sun was setting in Paiyu and it was beautiful.

The Paiyu campsite was a busy campground. There were many groups. There were some local Pakistani trekkers, Spanish team, Italian team, Polish team, and some Koreans. The foreigners were mainly serious climbers. One of them was the Luca. He was an Italian and had summited K2 in 2014. Nouman K., in our team was the most knowledgeable and sociable person, and he had used this rest day mingling with the majority of the teams camped in the Paiyu that day. Because of Nouman K. we were more informed on the peaks around us, stages ahead of us, and the other teams plans.

That night we had mutton curry for the dinner. By the way, we did have a pan-cooked vegetable pizza later that afternoon, which was quite a treat. In our meeting that night, Munna came with a proposal to do three stages next day to have an extra day at hand in case the weather get worst. On behalf of the other team, Munna suggested that we should go all the way to Urdukas skipping night stay at Khoburse. I initially agreed and voted to go all the way to Urdukas, and I couldn't wait to be at K2 base camp, the earlier the better. Nouman K. and Salman from our team raised some valid points. They said that they had seen how everyone struggled during the hike, and now that we would gain more height with the more treacherous terrain, most of the trekkers from the other team might not be able to catch up. There was a purpose for having these stages and these stages had been well planned out, Nouman K. and Salman pointed out. Their points were valid, and we insisted on sticking to the original tried and tested route.

Once all settled, we played card games and were in our sleeping bags by 10 p.m.

Figure 15: Top Left: Paiyu Peak, 6610 meters (21,686 ft.) (photo by
Salman Zakir); Top right: Searching for Trango Towers near Paiyu
Campsite; Bottom: Paiyu Campsite (photo by Salman Zakir)

8

DAY 4, PAIYU TO KHOBURSE – HELLO BALTORO

Around 4:45 a.m., I woke up with heavy breathing. Somehow my asthma had triggered. I was thirsty too and it was windy outside. I was reminded of the remoteness and roughness of such adventures. Among all this, Asim was snoring at his best. It was overall, a sleepless night for me. As valley warmed up during the sun rise, I started to feel better.

By 6:30 a.m., we were done with our standard breakfast, had packed our bags and were ready to leave for our next stage, Khoburse. We left the Paiyu campsite after our huddle prayers. After a mile or so we were on the Baltoro glacier. The Baltoro glacier, at 39 miles (63 km) long was one of the longest glaciers in the world and it can easily be spotted from the space as well. It was a "male" glacier in the local Balti slang. All the snow and ice was buried under sand and stones. When glaciers have all the snow and ice buried under sand and stones then Balti call them "male" glaciers. When the glaciers have exposed ice and snow then Balti call the glaciers "female". The Baltoro glacier was giving an impression of sand dunes made of brown rocks and brown mud. The formation was the same as a desert sand dunes with the exception of the river flowing under the dunes. The river came roaring out of the glacier and would disappear again in the glacier. We were at the tip of a terrain where glacier melts into the river. The Braldu Nala was narrower now. Lakes and large puddles were formed by more exposed parts of the glacier, and one can frequently hear rattling sound of the rocks randomly slipping into the lakes and the ponds. The trek was mostly close to such lakes, ponds, and ever dodging Braldu river. The trek would go up and down and would not remain constant and was getting slippery.

It was cloudy and windy and it started raining. We took out our waterproof jackets. The light but steady rain had made the trail muddy and slippery. The rocks would slip under our shoes and would plunge into the ravine. Initially, the trek was ascending and then it descended. Soon we were to cross the Braldu river. There was a point where the river was narrow and was swallowed by the glacier, and that's where we crossed to the other side. Now, the Braldu Nala would be on our left side whenever it surfaced again. The scary part was that after crossing, we had to cling to the wet trail to climb sharply. The furious but small river right under my feet was making me uncomfortable, but only way out was to move forward.

We took hints from the porters and followed their footsteps. The porters are born geniuses when it comes to crossing glaciers, rivers, and complex terrains. Their footing was perfect, and you would be amazed by the grip you would have and the distance you would cover with safety and comfort if you follow their footsteps as is. Some porters were kind to stop at exposed points and would lend a hand to inexperienced and unprepared trekkers like us.

After this steep climb, both glacier and valley widened, the Braldu Nala came out in the open and became wider. Now, we were trekking on white sand that sloped sharply into the Braldu Nala. We were still on the glacier and we felt as if we were in middle of a white desert with brown river ravaging through. The river disappeared under glacier again, and we descended again and did a sharp ascent. This ascent nearly killed us, but the views kept us alive. Now, we could see Trango Towers, Cathedral Peaks and some other peaks playing hide and seek with the clouds. At the ascent, we took a short break along with our porters, chit chatted a bit, recovered, and then hiked on. We finally made it to the Liligo stage. We were supposed to stop at Liligo stage, but there was no water, and we kept on marching. This surprise was a reminder that we should always carry extra water.

Are you from California?

At one turn through the trek, a lady trekker coming from other side asked "Who is Iftikar." I was surprised that my reputation had reached this far remote. I said "I am Iftikar." she then asked if I was from California. I said yes. She then said that there were people from California in her team. She pointed toward the other side of the trail. Before I could digest this and thanked her, the lady had disappeared. She looked non-Pakistani and was probably from Iran.

At the next turn, I saw two oncoming guys and I introduced myself and asked where they were from. To my pleasant surprise, they were from San Diego, California. I told them I was from San Francisco Bay Area, California. We all were ecstatic to see each other. We felt a connection right away, and we shared our experiences like buddies. They were returning from Concordia and said the weather was bad, and they couldn't do the Gondogoro pass. They were heading back the same route they came in. We took a selfie, wished each other luck, and parted our way. Even with Pakistan's current geopolitical situation, there were still people drawn to Pakistan's majestic mountain treasure. Meeting someone from my home state was a bonus and that was a real pleasure.

It turned out that Nouman K., who happened to be ahead of me, ran into those folks from the U.S. and told them about me and my U.S. connection. That's when the U.S. folks started asking trekkers on the trail "Who is Iftikar."

Made it to Khoburse Alive!

I entered the Khoburse site around 11:30 a.m., Nouman K. was with me, and Kashif as usual, was early and hugged us because he was not sure if we would make it alive. We had thought the same for him. We had done 8.18 miles that day. My average speed was 1.7 mph (miles per hour), and it took me five hours from Paiyu to the Khoburse.

The Khoburse campsite was at 12,441 feet of height. Khuborse, meaning "sour grass" in Balti language, had three stone hut rooms serving as seasonal canteen and storage room. The campsite was on a slope with sectioned out flat areas with stone boundaries. Our tents were pitched on one of the flat sectioned areas. We could see the Trango Towers and Cathedral Peaks from our tent. This was going to be the first camp night that made us feel as if we were on our way to something surreal.

There were no Italian style toilets. Toilets were waist-high stone walls with fifteen to twenty feet deep pits in the middle. You had to be very careful when you step inside those toilets. You don't want to fall twenty feet down into muddy poop. Sitting down and aiming right were the key to your survival. These were the best view toilets one can ever go, so no complaints there.

It was still raining on and off, and we were slightly wet. Salman, our teammate, befriended the canteen owner. Salman had found shelter in the canteen and was enjoying the green tea. He signaled us inside. The canteen was a small room and was warm. Salman's uncle had trekked to Concordia in the 1990's and his uncle's stories had inspired him into trekking. Salman was a seasoned trekker and had done most of the treks in Pakistan and always had interesting stories to tell. Salman was a good photographer and looked like the Indian film star Salman Khan. We named him Sallu Bhai right when we met him.

Late afternoon, weather cleared up a bit. Now, we could see Uli Biafo, Shipton Spire, Cathedral Peaks and Double Peak. Uli Biafo, 20,042 feet (6,109 meters), was named after an Italian climber who was the first to summit. Shipton Spire, 19,120 feet (5,828 meters) high, was named after the famous explorer who mapped Karakorum range and was the first one to summit the peak in 1934. Still there were clouds around Trango Towers. We would be able to see Trango Towers clearly tomorrow, weather permitting.

Trango Towers

I had mentioned Trango Towers many times so far. I think they deserve an introduction. Trango Towers were really big deal for me. I had been obsessed with them since I had seen their pictures many years ago. Trango Towers are the majestic, immense and forbidding walls of the world. They are the series of cliffs with the tallest vertical faces in the world. Highest tower has summit elevation of 20,623 ft. and has the vertical drop of 4,396 ft., which makes it officially the world's greatest nearly vertical drop in the extremes of the world. Trango Towers consist of Great Trango, Trango (nameless) Tower, Trango Monk, Trango II and Trango Ri are the prominent. Trango Towers are part of Baltoro-Muztagh range which is subrange of Karakoram range. Nameless Trango Tower is a very large pointed symmetrical spire which makes it more dominating of others. Trango Towers have their significance in rock climbing world.

These towers had been rarely climbed but these towers are rock climber's nirvana. Nameless Tower was last climbed by German rock climbers brothers Alexander and Thomas Huber in 2009. Most recently Nameless Tower was climbed by two Pakistani rock climbers, Imran Junaidi and Usman Tariq in 2014. So far these are the only Pakistanis who have summited Trango Tower. Trango Towers are considered most difficult to climb due to altitude, steepness of the rocks, and total heights of the rocks.

Trango Towers were mentioned in a Hollywood movie "Point Break" where it was discussed as one of the possible locations for a task by the extreme adventure athletes to honor forces of nature. In 1992, two Australians, Nic Feteris and Glenn Singlman climbed Great Trango and BASE jumped (body parachute jump) from elevation of 19,537 ft. and landed into Dunge Glacier at 13,779 ft., setting the highest BASE jumping record in the world at that time. This record has been beaten since then. Thanks to BASE jumping from Everest by Valery Rozov in 2013.

The Late Comers

By late afternoon, we were in our mess tent. The other team had not yet reached the campsite. We were concerned for the late comers. We were done in five hours, and it was more than ten hours for some. Our guide, Ibrahim Munna, arrived at Khoburse around 5 p.m. He had injured his hand. He got some scratches on his hand while trying to help a trekker ascend a hill. "He was too fat" Munna exclaimed. Munna didn't seem pleased. He was concerned for the remaining trekkers, who hadn't arrived yet. He then sent some of the porters with some tea to help out remaining nine trekkers who were too slow and too behind.

I thought there should be some criteria for people to join the team. The unprepared not only made their trip miserable, they made other suffer too. This trek was tough. It started raining again. I felt bad for the trekkers who were still somewhere in the glacier. Around 7:30 p.m., we were done with dinner, rice, vegetables, leftover mutton curry, garlic, and onion

We then noticed that the other remaining trekkers also made it to the campsite. It was not a pleasant sight watching them walk into the campground. They were in excruciating pain and didn't care about the scenery the campsite had to offer. They just wanted to survive and end this. Thank goodness we didn't go all the way to Urdukas as they had suggested. They would had to trek in the night and the rain on the unforgiving glacier if they had attempted to go all the way to Urdukas. They were first timers with not much or no trekking background. A team with members having similar experience helps a lot and decisions made are usually smarter and efficient. A mixed bag of people with little or no trekking history could put others at risk. We saw that first hand.

Figure 16: Top left: A sand rock formation on Baltoro Glacier; Top right: A sand-rock formation along with makeshift lake, Balotoro Glacier; Bottom: Braldu Nala emerging from the mouth of Balotor Glacier

Figure 17: Top left: Our cook, Imran, taking break on Paiyu-Khoburse trail; Top right: A selfie with homies from California, Paiyu-Khoburse trail; Bottom: Always changing Paiyu-Khoburse trail on Baltoro Glacier

Figure 18: Top left: Ulli Biafo Tower, 6109 meters (20,043 ft.) as seen from Khoburse Campsite; Top right: Khoburse Campsite; Bottom: Porters resting in their plastic makeshift tent; (photos by Salman Zakir)

9

DAY 5, KHOBURSE TO URDUKUS – EASY PEASY

I woke up 4:30 a.m., the sky was clear and the winds had taken the clouds away. I could see all the peaks loud and clear. Trango Towers were clearly visible. It was priceless amazing!

Around 7 a.m., we were ready to leave. The temperature was freezing, 40 degrees Fahrenheit. The sun was up and shining on half of the valley now. We were a little cold, huddled when ready, said our prayers, and left the Khoburse campsite.

For one hour, the trek was same as the day before so we were kind of prepared. We then came across a "female" glacier on right merging into the Baltoro Glacier. Remember that female glacier is the white icy, snowy glacier with no sand and stone toppings. It was a few hundred yards wide, and we had to trek on the ice. After some ascent on the ice we then descended into a small dip, crossed a stream in the glacier, and then came across our first crevasse on our path. It was a beauty and the beast at the same time. We took some pictures of crevasse and continued. Trek widened after that, and we were able to see the tip of Broad Peak. Cathedral, Uli Biafo, and Trango Towers were still in clear view. Broad Peak was our first glimpse of an eight-thousander. Broad Peak, the twelfth highest in the world, stood tall and wide high at 26,414 feet (8,051 meters) ahead of us.

It was easy an trek until we reached the last stretch of the Urdukas campsite. It was a five hundred to six hundred feet sharp ascent through green bushes and plants. This stretch was a little strenuous but it was a welcome change. It reminded us of pleasant hike among green alpine meadows, tough but pleasant. It was a clay trek with green bushes, with no rocks, just an uphill climb.

Urdukas

We reached the Urdukas campsite in two hours. It was only 3.5 total hiking miles that day. The Urdukas campsite at 13,317 feet was surprisingly green. There were no trees, and it was on a slope with layered sections for the camps. At the edge of the slope, there was a big rock stretching out to the valley. Urdukus means a big fallen rock in the Balti language. There was a multi-story high big rock at one end which had one corner hung over the Baltoro Glacier. That rock's top was a popular hangout area for the porters. We hiked to that rock and enjoyed the incredible vistas. Down below one could see the Baltoro glacier spread across in the valley. The glacier looked like a wide wavy frozen river covered with sand and stones. No more sign of the Braldu Nala. We could see tiny streams flowing through the glacier in only a few places.

It was 9:30 a.m., and we had the entire day ahead of us in the Urdukas. The temperature was approximately eighty degrees Fahrenheit due to the bright direct sun. There were some Italian toilets at some distance. We grabbed the bucket and a pan and took turns for a shower. It was one hour past noon, so we survived glacier water shower.

There was the army check post few hundreds of yards ahead. We went there. Check post was nothing but three plastic Igloos and a flag pole with a Pakistan flag on it. We chatted with the only army Jawan there. He was from the small town Khushab, Punjab. He had been at this post for last three months, had no contact with family at all and had six more months to spend there before he would be going home. He was a tall, slim young guy with thick Punjabi accent.

I noticed a lot of pretty white butterflies. Flies were plenty too. The Trango Towers were very clear and bright. We all sat on the dominating hanging rock and stared at Trango Towers and other peaks for hours. At 3 p.m., we were called into our mess tent and were served French Fries and *pakoras* (an all time favorite Pakistani fried snack made by deep frying gram flour coated vegetables). We charged the *pakoras* and wiped cleaned our plates. It was such a treat.

The sun was bright, and it was burning on us. Our lips were still dry even after applying lip balm after lip balm. It was dusty in the later afternoon. I was asking myself why I was doing this. Too much idle time. Oh, and we also treated some porters with their injuries. They had minor cuts and pains, but nothing as severe as we encountered before.

Antoine Girard's High Altitude Paragliding

Nouman K., Asim, and I sat on the big rock overhanging the Baltoro glacier. The views were fantastic, and we were spellbound. Nouman K. pointed towards the sky and said, "look there is something up there, and it's moving." With some effort, I was able to zoom onto that thing. It was a yellow dot at the height of 26,000 feet or probably higher. I thought someone might be parachuting. But that yellow object maintained its altitude and moved toward the Broad Peak and made a circle on the Broad Peak and disappeared. Nouman K. said someone must be doing high altitude paragliding. It was unbelievable. Nouman K.'s guess was correct, and we later found out that it was the mountaineer Antoine Girard and he indeed did do paragliding that day over the Broad peak and the Baltoro Glacier. Antoine Girard had shared his paragliding videos on his YouTube page. We found that out when Shami shared Antoine's video link on Facebook after the trip. The video is an absolute stunner. Anyone can search Antoine Girard on YouTube and feast on those amazing videos.

We then walked around the the Urdukas campsite. Some porters had taken shelter under large rocks and were cooking their meals. They had to carry their own food in addition to the load they were required to haul. A few years ago, a large rock had lost its footing and rolled over the porters who were sitting under it taking refuge from the pouring rain. The rock had killed them all in an instant. We also came across a makeshift memorial of the fallen climbers. The late climbers name and the date of their death was hand carved into silver metal plates.

We then saw some guys from other team doing some rock climbing on the large rock hanging over the Baltoro Glacier. Those climbers looked professional and were doing some warm up practices.

Urdukas Almost Got Me

The temperature dropped to 55 degrees Fahrenheit from 90 degrees Fahrenheit as soon as sun disappeared behind the Trango Towers. In dinner, we had pasta that night. We also invited the Jawan from the post to join us for dinner. He was not a big fan of pasta but he was a good sport. After dinner, some of us went out and laidd down under the open sky and gazed at the stars. It was a different Urdukas at night. Everything had changed; the stars were bright lit like someone had frozen the fireworks and scattered them across the sky.

After the stargazing, I was in my tent around 8 p.m. I didn't remember when I fell asleep. Very late at night, I had terrible rumblings in my stomach, and I knew I had to go the toilet ASAP. *Pakoras* had done their magic. It was freezing. I grabbed the headlamp and headed out. The water streams were frozen due to the low temperature but luckily Asim had some water in his bottle in the tent. I couldn't find the toilet paper, so I stole his bottle while he was busy snoring.

The toilets were hundreds of yards away and were on the slopes. The trail was narrow and had steep drops to the Baltoro Glacier hundreds of feet below. I cringed and carefully took step at a time. It was dark and the trail was dangerous. Night creatures were out, and where my headlamp beam the light, I saw lizards and other reptiles crawling. Luckily, those night creatures were averse to the light and crawled away from the trail as my headlamp's light shined on them.

It was cold and the pressure to relieve myself was increasing by the second. I rushed and tried to walk fast, but it had become very discomforting by every step I took in that night. I was concerned what will people say in my eulogy in case I fell off the cliff. They would say "Last time we saw him he was heading towards toilet with a bottle in his hand."

I made it. I survived the night in the beautiful Urdukas.

Figure 19: Top left: Hanging rock of the Urdukus Campsite; Top right: Great Trango of Trango Towers, 6,286 meters (20,623 ft.), as seen from Urdukus Campsite; Bottom: Chilling with the porters at the hanging rock of Urdukus Campsite. Lobsang Spire, 5707 meters, in background; (photos by Salman Zakir)

Figure 20: Top left: Memorial plates of the fallen; Top right: Memorial plates of the fallen; Bottom: Urdukus Campsite overlooking Baltoro Glacier; (photos by Nouman K.)

Figure 21: Top left: Chilling next to our tent at Urdukus Campsite; Top right: Our kitchen tent and mess tent at Urdukus Campsite; Bottom: Tents at Urdukus Campsite overlooking Baltoro Glacier and surrounding peaks; (photos by Salman Zakir)

Figure 22: Top Left: Main Cathedral Peak 6,024 meters (19,764 ft.); Top right: Paiyu Peak, 6610 meters (21,686 ft.), as seen from Khoburse Campsite; Bottom: Trango Towers as seen from Urdukus Campsite; (photos by Salman Zakir)

10

DAY 6, URDUKAS TO GORE II - THIS IS NOT MARRIOT

I woke up around four in the morning. We were done with breakfast and were going to leave in an hour. It was a cold morning, I had three layers on me and in addition I had to wear gloves. When the sun would come up then things would warm up, but for now, it was freezing.

Munna Ibrahim, our lead guide, had his assistants served breakfast to other team separately. When Munna's kitchen team packed up, a request for another round of breakfast from that team. Some of their member had woken up late. Munna Ibrahim had it by that time. He went off like a cannon and went on a long rant. Munna didn't have the luxury to open the kitchen during odd hours. He said blatantly that this was not the Marriott.

Munna was entirely justified, and it was the sixth day, and some people would not tone down on their unusual requests, despite the fact that they would see how hard the porters and staff were working and how challenging and remote the territory was. All the porters and helpers were very kind and would always go extra miles yet there were always some people who would ask for things non-stop. I had noted that earlier and was critical of them. Our team had shown more maturity and treated our helpers and porters with more respect. Simple things such as saying thanks would make their day.

"This is not Marriot" became a catchy phrase and we used this phrase to poke fun at each other whenever somebody asked for something that others deemed unusual.

We left the Urdukas around 6:30 a.m. We walked past the Pakistan Army Igloo checkpoint and were greeted by a Jawan. He shook our hand and wished us luck with a big warm smile.

Today we were supposed to do two stages. We would rest at stage Gore-I and then march to Gore-II for the night stay, skipping Gore-I. The terrain was the same as the day before, but the views had changed. The valley had opened up, and the Baltoro Glacier was wider than before. There was no sign of Braldu Nala, it was all under the glacier and was in the form of small scattered streams. There were "female" glaciers from the side mountains merging into the Baltoro glacier. Merging glaciers made impressive slopes and exposed more crevasses.

The air was getting thinner, and it was getting harder to breathe. The weather was clear and it was getting warmer and drier as the day progressed. The glacier was still sand dunes like formation, and we were steadily ascending and then descending. We would drop into dips only to ascend again. When the army Jawan at the Urdukas had pointed out the Gore-II campsite from the rock in Urdukas, Gore-II looked near and downhill. In reality, it was not near and certainly not downhill. Maybe it was because of the clear air that we could see things clearly in the distance and the earth's curve was giving us the optical illusion that Gore-II was downhill. It would be hours and hours before we could be even close to Gore-II.

Gore-I

It was 4.7 miles from Urdukas to Gore-I. Gore-I was a no shade stop area on the Baltoro Glacier. It was just a resting point, and there was no water. I guessed since it was the midpoint, everyone stopped for a quick break. Fast trekkers waited up for the slower ones. Glacier was wider and ice was more exposed, still mostly rocky, though. It gave the feeling of walking on a thick slush of ice and rock. There were crevasses and ice cones. I could see loud and clear: the Masherbrum Peak, 25,659 feet (7,821 meters) high, also called K1 and is the 22nd highest peak of the world. The peak G-IV, 25,987 feet (7,921 meters), the 17th highest peak of the world stood like a tall pyramid at the trail end, as if blocking our trail.

Soon Gore-I became a picnic spot. Porters unpacked cooking gear and cooked local tea known as Tumbrook. Tumbrook was made from local herbs, abundantly available near trails at certain points. Porters collected Tumbrook leaves on their way. It was guaranteed fresh and completely organic. We sat on rocks and had dry apricots, biscuits, and tea. We had great discussions, and vented with the porters.

A stream was dividing the glacier. It was a stream running through the ice bed and the ice walls. The stream would converge into a dark crevasse and then it would disappear and flow into the crevasse. The stream was a few hundred feet down on our right side. It was both beautiful and scary at the same time.

Got Lost?

While on our way to Gore-II, I felt like I was walking on a different planet. There was nothing that I could relate with that I had experienced before. I was immersed in the landscape, listening to the random sounds of rocks rattling, soaking in soothing thin air, and tuning in to low notes of stream whenever it surfaced. Nouman K., ten yards ahead of me, was tuned to his iPhone music. While his earphones pumped music into his ear he kept walking and I kept following him. I tend to stick close to the hiker whom I can match my hiking pace comfortably. But, neither of us realized that were way off from the trail and each step was taking us farther away.

Nouman K. stopped close to a drop and I stopped behind him because we could no longer continue. "I swear, I saw some tents in this direction." He exclaimed. He explained his rationale behind taking this route. He wanted to continue in the same direction by-passing the drops. My counter rationale was that we hadn't seen a porter or any trekker for some time so we were definitely lost and definitely going in wrong direction. There was no trail on the glacier that we could trek back on. There rocks all over. It was like getting lost in the desert of rocks on ice.

I suggested that we should not move unless we were sure of which way to go. It must be the Army's supplier abandoned tents that Nouman might had mistook for Gore-II campsite. Luckily, I had a whistle in my back pack which I could use to whistle for help. In this quiet valley whistle sound could cover lot of square miles area. A very light weight whistle could be our life saver. Nouman and I started to scout the area. We climbed couple of rock-ice dunes to spot porters or trekkers but no luck.

I spotted a chocolate wrapper. Somebody had conveniently left his or her legacy behind for posterity. It was definitely a foreigner trekker as the chocolate wrapper was of a chocolate not available in Pakistan. Then I saw a *nimko* (a popular snack in Pakistan) wrapper. Baltoro glacier was being littered without any discrimination. These wrappers could have flown away from the trail so they were no guaranteed indicators of the right direction. It was a good 30 minutes before I spotted a faraway porter emerged from a dune and then disappeared into another dune. That was our clue. Nouman and I rushed toward that dune and caught up with the porter. We were finally back on route to Gore-II.

Finally, we reached Gore-II campsite without any dramatic incident. Most of the trekkers had already arrived. Nouman tried to tell the team that we got lost but nobody cared. They thought we were giving excuse for being slow.

Gore-II

The Gore-II campsite was 14,070 feet high and was 2.43 miles from the Gore-I. It was almost two hours of trek, 370 feet gain and 155 feet descent. The Baltoro Kangri Peak, 25,334 feet (7,722 meters), could be seen wide open on our left. I felt dizzy at times due to altitude and exhaustion.

There were two Italian toilets of a different style than we had seen at Jhola and Paiyu. They were built on a steel platform with steel stairs. The platform had a square hole and a blue drum attached under the hole. The light brown canvas was used as walls for privacy. With the world class views nobody complained. You needed to point and shoot in that small square hole with the attached blue drum. CKNP staff maintained the blue drums. All the toilets and their maintenance was done with the financial support from the Italians. So, thank you Italy.

The same porter whom we treated at Burdumal for the first-degree burn came to us for follow-up. Nouman K. and I changed his bandage. I acted as Nouman's assistant and supplied the bandages. We were relieved to see that he was healing. Kudos to Nouman for the courage to clean his wounds and bandage him.

That night we were camping on the glacier. Porters built themselves waist high wall rooms of stone. They then used the plastic sheet as a roof. They would cook their bread with locally grown wheat. They would also make Tumbrook tea and black milk tea with lots of salt in it. The porters would then huddle together in their warm makeshift houses with a transparent plastic roof that trapped the heat inside. They would have tea and bread and would pass the cold glacier night.

We all decided to sleep in our mess tent instead of our regular dome like sleeping tents. We used all of the mattresses that we could legitimately collect to shield against the glacier ice. Doubling up the mattresses helped but the mess tent was too tight for seven people and Asim's snoring was like rubbing salt in our wounds. Someone asked for an extra mattress, and we reacted "This is not Marriott!"

Again, discussion of going directly to K2 Basecamp came up. Due to the severe weather warnings, it was getting more likely that we would not have a rest day at Concordia. As per our plans, a rest day at Concordia was supposed to give us the opportunity to have a day trip to go to the K2 Basecamp and back. So one option was to go directly to the K2 Basecamp from Gore-II, spend some time at basecamp and trek back to Concordia to spend the night. K2 Basecamp was one stage ahead of Concordia. So it would be three stages if we would directly go to the K2 Basecamp. One stage to go to Concordia and then one stage to K2 Basecamp and then one stage back to Concordia. As per Munna, it was at least ten hours of trekking, but for us, it could be easily fifteen hours in the high altitude. Not too many people were excited about that idea. However, I was determined to go all the way. I didn't want to miss out on K2 Basecamp. I was secretly hoping that weather warning might fade away, but so far warnings were being confirmed by all possible sources and that day was my only shot to K2 Basecamp.

Munna agreed to our idea of going directly to K2 Basecamp, but it was optional. Only Kashif, Saad, and I committed to taking the chance. Munna agreed to assign a porter to our mini team to take us to K2 Basecamp and bring us back to Concordia campsite.

Figure 23: Left: Porters resting at Khoburse-Gore II trail, G-IV in the background; Top right: Khoburse-Gore II trail on the Baltoro Glacier; Bottom Right: Khoburse-Gore II trail; (photos by Salman Zakir)

Figure 24: Top left: Porters taking rest at Liligo Stage (photo by Salman Zakir); Top right: Team taking pseudo lunch break at Liligo (photo by Nouman K.); Bottom: A lone trekker on Khuborse-Gore II trail (photo by Nouman K.)

Figure 25: All: Variation of Khoburse-Gore II trail on Baltoro Glacier;
(photos by Salman Zakir)

Figure 26: Top Left: An Italian toilet at Gore-II Campsite with views of G-IV Peak; Top right: G-IV Peak, 7,925 meters (26,001 ft.); Bottom: Gore-II Campsite in late afternoon; (photos by Salman Zakir)

11

DAY 7, GORE-II TO CONCORDIA - THE BEST VIEWS

At 5:45 a.m., Kashif, Saad, Yaseen and I, were on the trek to the Concordia campsite. Saad was a young lad with aspirations to join the Pakistan soccer team. Since the start of trekking Saad has spent most of his time in the kitchen tent however he was a fast trekker. It was hard to catch up with him. Yaseen was our porter cum guide for that day. Chacha Yassen, as we called him, was seasoned and I guessed he was in his late forties or early fifties. Allow me to digress here a bit. *Chacha* means uncle in Urdu language. In Pakistani culture, it is perfectly okay to address anybody as your relative as long as respect is intended. For example, *chacha, taya* and *mamoo,* all mean uncle and you can use any of these titles to any person you deem appropriate.

Four of us left earlier because we wanted to go all the way to the K2 Basecamp. There were severe weather warnings, and we would not get a chance to go to base camp next day. It was an uphill challenge, our estimated trekking time for that day was ten hours and we were up for it.

Chacha Yaseen had 25 kilos on him, and we had just the day packs on our backs. It was Chacha Yassen's backyard. He was breezing through, and we were barely catching up. The terrain was almost the same, but views were opening up. We could see a junction way ahead of us making a T. When we were into two and half hours of trekking then came the best part. We could then glimpse a side of the K2 for the first time. It was just a side of the K2 but it was enormous and very dominating. It was quite a treat. We wondered how magical would it be when we would get close to it.

It was 7.52 miles to Concordia from Gore-II. It took us approximately three and half hours. We started at 14,000 feet and ended at Concordia at approximately 15,000 feet. During trekking, there was an elevation loss of 400 feet. And we gained 1300 feet. This trek took a toll on me. Going from 14,000 to 15,000 feet in three and half hours sucked the energy out of me. Those seven and half miles drained me out. The altitude sucked energy out of my legs like a vacuum cleaner sucks dust on a floor.

Concordia

By 8:30 a.m., we were at the Concordia campsite. The Concordia campsite, at the height of 14,967 feet, sits at the confluence of three mighty glaciers of the world known as Baltoro, Godwin-Austen, and Vigne. This site offers the best views of the best peaks of the world. If there were a mountain god, then definitely Concordia would be the mountain god's throne, hands down. I could imagine the Greek God Zeus having a council here, discussing matters with Jupiter, Apollo, Hera, Helen, and all other Gods. Maybe the Gods from Homer's classic, the Iliad, sat here directing war of Troy.

This place was magical. I could see a wall of peaks after peaks. And these peaks were no ordinary peaks. These were the eight-thousander and seven-thousander peaks. Pakistan have five eight-thousanders and four of them can be seen from here or accessed from here at Concordia. Seven-thousander peaks are 7,000 meters (23,000 ft.) and higher. Their height was not the only thing to brag about them, they also were the beauties. We could see the K2, 28,251 feet (8,611 meters) high loud and clear. Also visible were Broad Peak, 26,414 feet (8,051 meters), G-II, 26,362 feet (8,035 meters), G-III, 26,089 feet (7,952 meters), G-IV, 26,001 feet (7,925 meters), Saltoro Kangri, 25,400 feet (7,742 meters), Mitre Peak, 19,720 feet (6,010 meters) and many other peaks were clearly visible. All those peaks mixed with the mighty glaciers made this place look like the throne of mountain gods.

Under the shadow of these mighty peaks, the three mighty glaciers Baltoro, Godwin-Austen and Vigne looked like a curving freeway of ice with the busy traffic of thick mud, dark chocolate stones, and coffee dunes. The different texture of snow, ice, mud, and stone gives an impression of a busy multiple lanes freeway.

There were many other teams already camped there. We could see two toilets on a raised platform with blue drums on our left. At Concordia, we could see clusters of colorful tents spread throughout the dark brown and black stones covering the Baltoro Glacier. There were many teams camped there, and the team porters were roaming around. Chacha Yaseen found a spot and left his load with a porter he knew he could trust. We had a break of thirty minutes to catch up on our breaths. Munna had packed us *paratha* and egg omelet rolls.

To K2 Basecamp

After a short break, we left theConcordia campsite for the Broad Peak Basecamp. Trek was almost nonexistent, and the glacier was wilder than before. Only Chacha Yaseen, our seasoned porter, would know where to go. There were slopes dropping into crevasses and there were makeshift lakes. It was a maze of small peaks of stones with sharp drops to the exposed ice crevasses and snowy lakes.

We had been trekking for half an hour or so, and that was when I started having trouble breathing. I couldn't maintain my composure, and I was missing steps, and I was dizzy. At few points, I rescued myself from stepping into crevasses. I was under the spell of these mountains now, and they were casting a curse on me. I was mesmerized, and at the same time, my basic survival instinct told me that something was out. I sat down holding my head with my hands while the rest of the gang kept marching on. I regained strength and composure and took few more steps and then collapsed. I knew it was altitude and exhaustion that were holding me down. I could think of myself all I could, but the body has its limit. I had hit that limit there and I knew that.

I attempted to walk a few more times and collapsed to the ground again. Looking at the drops at both sides, I signaled to Kashif and Saad to stop. When I caught up with them, I told them the situation, and they instantly decided to pause than to be sorry. They were quite content for where they were. K2 was clearly visible in front of us and what else we could have wished. We decided to take an extended break and then see if things could turn around. We paused our activities for some time, but that did not help my condition at all. We had to be back before sunset and we still had to cover lot of miles. I was the one who couldn't keep up the pace and had let the team down. I was disappointed, really disappointed. Shame on me, I lamented.

Kashif was cool with it. He said he didn't care where we headed, he just wanted to accompany me. Saad said this was the best view ever. He further said people spend weeks here just to take a peek at the K2 and we were extremely lucky that we could see it all loud and clear on our very first day. Saad poured his words of wisdom: "we are lucky and blessed and let us cherish that." "Let's not kill ourselves," he further said. I was impressed by Saad's theory and it helped me console a bit.

We found a picture perfect spot in front of the K2. We took pictures and savored the moment. We made videos, selfies, and all that. We got excited and took shirtless pictures. We were there and we wanted to celebrate. For the most part, we just stared at the K2, mesmerized, bowing to its beauty.

After spending hours, we marched back to the Concordia campsite. I was turning back frequently and checking out K2. Physically, I was getting worse, and the trek was challenging. We were in the middle of the glacier, with lots of tricky ups and downs. We made it back in an hour or so. Munna Ibrahim got worried as he saw me walking into the Concordia campsite. Munna was a fast reader of the situation. He immediately summoned me to kitchen tent and asked me to lie down. He then gave me garlic cloves to eat. Garlic cloves are a magic antidote to altitude issues, and it was a tried and tested Balti medicine. I have no problems with garlic but that time garlic tasted weird, due to my condition, but I swallowed it little by little. Munna would give me more garlic cloves and peeled onions. Given the attention, I realized that I was in terrible shape and we probably made the right call to return on time.

Back to Concordia

My entire day was spent in kitchen tent eating garlic cloves and recovering. In addition, I inhaled plenty of kerosene oil fumes from the nearest cooking stove. While lying on the kitchen tent floor I made sure that I lied down in a direction facing the magnificent K2 such that whenever I muster enough energy to open my eyes I would look at the K2. All of my team went out on a phot shoot frenzy. They would come to tent and would try to woo me to come out of the tent. All I remember was the shadows coming to tent, whispering something and then disappearing onto the Baltoro Glacier, as if pulled away by the magnetic super powers of the K2. It was not until the late afternoon that spell on me starting to fall apart.

Later I was told that that late afternoon our team had meeting in which next day's plans were discussed. As per

Munna, there were severe weather warnings, and he wanted the group to be out of there as soon as possible. These weather warnings were confirmed by the Spanish team, who were also planning to get out of the Concordia as soon as possible. Earlier we had met a team who had camped in Ali camp for two nights to find an opening to cross Gondogoro La, but they had to return to the Concordia, and they headed back to Askole via Baltoro Glacier.

Munna had seen bad weather and knew dangers it can bring. Munna and his team were anxious for our safety. Munna would lay out all the possible scenarios. He didn't sugar coat possible outcome of our suggestions. As per him, it was best for the group to head for Gondogoro La the very next day. We shouldn't wait at all. We had to let go the rest day at Concordia to better our odds of doing Gondogoro La.

We were supposed to have a rest day at the Concordia, but that also meant we could risk our Gondogoro La route. If we have to skip the Gondogoro La, we would have to go back the same way as we came in and none of us wanted that. Doing the Gondogoro La was challenging and risky however it could save us three days. The Gondogoro La would lead us into the Hushe valley. The new route would give us a new experience, new views, and lesser days, so it was preferred. The only thing that stood between us and the better route was the Gondogoro mountain range. Gondogoro mountain range was like a wall of snow rock mountains stitched together sitting at around 20,000 feet high. There was a path between these peaks at approximately 19,500 feet with a steep ascent and steep descent, known as Gondogoro La. Ropes were installed to facilitate the climb and descend of the Gondogoro La. Above all, there was a limited time window during which crossing of Gondogoro La could be attempted.

Based on weather consideration we decided to head out to Gondogoro La early next morning thus leaving the Concordia after spending only one night there. A few team members from other group were to drop out from the Gondogoro La route and were to return via the same route that we came in, that is Goro-II, Urdukas, etc. to Askole. Those team members had run out of steam and the physical strength and had reached a point where they could easily put their lives in danger. Their physical condition had put porters, and guides on edge. The guides and helpers also refused to take responsibility to watch out for the slow and the amateurs. The porters and the guides had been helping them all along, but Gondogoro was a different game. It was the survival of the fittest.

We enjoyed rest of the evening walking in and around the Concordia campsite. Beautiful and magical views were all around us. We didn't comment or talk about anything we just watched. Sunset was amazingly different. Half of the K2 was in the shade and the other half was bright yellow with dying sunlight.

Shami expressed a strong desire to trek into one of the large crevasses to take pictures of curvy, blue water flowing through the crevasse with a view of the K2 in the background and possibly stars. He was determined, and he packed himself into warm clothing and headed out into the night. Munna asked Chacha Yaseen to accompany Shami. Munna wouldn't let Shami go alone for safety reasons. Shami spent many hours into the night trying to capture the best shot. Eventually, he was able to find a perfect spot. Right when he was to click the camera button, lo and behold his camera battery died! He returned to the campsite late that night with a long sad face.

Later when we found out about Shami's battery miss adventure, we expressed our sorrow. Once he calmed down we started making fun of him like friends do. We had to do what we were good at, that was making fun. We were expecting that Shami would throw tantrums to express frustration on that missed opportunity but rather he showed content that he was back at the Concordia campsite without any harm. Apparently, he and Chacha Yaseen were lost and had to struggle to come back to the campsite in the dark. Shami was little disappointed, though. Chacha Yaseen had slipped and scratched his legs against the boulders.

At the Concordia, we were served with refreshing *pakoras* and French Fries with the ketchup, again. To counter any reaction of *pakoras* late that night, I kept my filled water bottle with me during sleep time. I also charted out the shortest route to the nearest toilet, and kept mental notes. Luckily there were no steep drops on the way to the toilets so at least I would not be afraid of disappearing in the Baltoro Glacier for good.

Let me fill you in our plans for next day. Our plan was to trek to the Ali Camp in the morning. We would be in Ali Camp by noon if things went well. We would spend the day resting, and in the night around 9 p.m., we would head out to the Muneer Camp, which was one hour up from Ali camp. We would then rest at the Muneer Camp for 15-20 minutes and then start our ascent to the Gondogoro La using ropes. The ascent would take all night. We would be at the top by the wee hours of the morning and then after a quick break, we would start our descent and continue trekking until we had reached the Khushpang Campsite. If all went okay, then we were supposed to be at the Khushpang around noon. Sounds like a plan!

Figure 27: Top left: Angel Peak, 6,858 meters (22,500 ft.); Top right: K2 Peak, 8,611 meters (28,251 ft.), as seen from Concordia; Bottom: Asim, Shami, Nauman S., Voila, Andrew and Nouman K at Concorda, K2 in the background; (photos by Salman Zakir)

Figure 28: Top Left: Broad Peak, 8,051 meters (26,414 ft.), as seen from Concordia (photo by Nouman K.); Top right: Miter Peak, 6,070 meters (19,915 ft.), as seen from Concordia (photo by Salman Zakir); Bottom: Concordia Campsite as seen from Gore-II-Concordia trail (photo by Salman Zakir)

Figure 29: Top Left: Kashif and Ifti celebrating with attitude at the altitude; Right: Ifti styling like Bolt near K2; Bottom Left: Our team, from left; Salman, Saad, Asim, Nauman S., Munna, Nouman K., Shami, Ifti & Kashif

12

DAY 8, CONCORDIA TO THE GONDOGORO CAMPS

I woke up around 5 a.m. with shortness of breath. I had a good sleep, but it's the morning that triggered something. My head was heavy, and it looked like altitude sickness was still haunting me. I peeked out of the tent, I could only see the clouds and nothing else. Clouds had blanketed up all the peaks around us, and even K2 was in hiding. It was cold, below freezing, I guessed. I put on the base layer, my UV (Ultra Violet) protected shirt, outer shell, beanie, and gloves. The weather warnings were turning out to be true, and we had only that day to make it to the Gondogoro La.

Concordia was a busy campsite, and there were many professional teams camped there. Some were up for Broad Peak, some had teams at K2 Basecamp, some were eyeing G-II summit, some were aiming for Gondogoro La like us and some were just getting ready to return to Askole via Baltoro Glacier. Also, there was an army of porters, guides, and cooks. For them, it was just another day at work.

For Munna, being our lead guide, this was a difficult day.

He had to let go of the porters who were contracted to carry weight until the Concordia campsite. After all, the food was consumed, and some porters had no loads to haul. The trek becomes trickier for the mules after the Concordia, so the mules had to be turned around. Munna had to split the rations between the teams who were returning via Baltoro and the team who was doing Gondogoro La. For Gondogoro La, porters could only carry eighteen kilos, so Munna had to decide which items he could let go with the other porters to Askole.

While Munna was busy making such arrangements, we, the trekkers packed up and were taking final pictures. The other team guy, the *shehri babu* group lead, asked us to be part of his team picture. We knew he wanted to advertise his team as larger team to attract more trekking customers later. We showed good sportsmanship and didn't object. That group photo later showed up on Facebook with his company logo. No surprise there.

The K2 Peak was still playing hide and seek, but now the sun was also making an entry. So it was a stunning beautiful morning. Munna gave us a briefing and told us that the first hour of trek would be tough and it was mandatory to follow our guides instructions for our safety.

Concordia to Ali Camp via Vigne Glacier, the most scenic freeway

If you were to take the set of freeways and runways in the world and freeze them, it would look like a Vigne glacier. Now add K2 at one end, Broad Peak, G-II, G-IV et al. on sides and a wall of mountains on the other side. Also, throw in a forty three miles long Baltoro Glacier in the mix. The landscape was totally out of the world. This place could have easily been on another planet, and it was just so unearthly. Vigne glacier was the white glacier that spawns out Godwin-Austen glacier, which was dark gray and curves slight right to the K2. And there was Baltoro glacier that starts right where

Godwin-Austen and Vigne glacier meet. How can one describe that landscape, I knew I could not.

At 7 a.m., we started hiking out of Concordia, and we were to turn right and then had our backs to K2. But first, we needed to cross a set of the major open crevasses that we were afraid to go near. We followed a line of porters. Our designated guide was Iqbal, a tall humble guy. He watched us like a hawk and stood on small crevasse's opening, would lend his hand "Sir, do not step on it, it's a crevasse." He held my hand and helped me jump over the crevasse. I couldn't help but notice that he was wearing thick blue plastic slippers, not more than sandals worth a dollar, and thick old socks, yet he had such a good grip on the glacier that it would put us to shame. I was appalled at his control and balance yet I thought he should at least have better shoes. He spends more time in glaciers in a single season than any of us trekkers would spend in our lifetimes.

Then there came a tricky part where we were to cross two glacier streams that were running in parallel. We walked on a narrow icy ridge with both the streams on both the sides. The streams had a shade of blue and were magical. The ice and snow around the streams composed good rhythmic flow of glacial water as if a musician orchestrated the symphony. The narrow icy ridge that we were balancing on had gaps that we would jump over and had sharp ascents and descents with drops at both sides to the streams. I was not sure where one would end up if one fell. We walked on that treacherous ridge for few hundreds of yards, and at one point the blue stream disappeared into the glacier, which gave us a narrow patch spot to cross it. In all that, the slanting mystical Mitre Peak was right in front of us. The Broad Peak and the dashing K2 were on our backs.

Once we crossed the bold and beautiful glacier streams, we were on a terrain on which boulders were scattered everywhere on top of snow and ice. There were some frozen puddles visible. We were advised not step on any frozen puddle, because it was not known how deep that little pool would be and or could it be just a tip of a crevasse. This rolling glacier was like a plateau with rolling hills. There were ups and downs, and we were taking on one boulder at a time.

It was still cloudy, but the sun was blasting away clouds. Now, K2 was visible, I had taken off the jacket and was comfortable walking in my full sleeve shirt and a base layer, I kept the beanie and gloves on, though. The views were unbeaten. It was the throne of the mountains gods, after all. We had to be respectful and bow our heads while we humbly crunched ice under our shoes.

We were into the second hour of trekking and now boulders were giving way to ice and snow. We were now more on ice and snow than on rocks. There was constant crunching sound under our feet. Now, we were running into more crevasses than before. Thanks to the porters ahead of us we could easily follow tracks to the safe point to cross such cracks. After some time the ice and snow widened. Now, small smooth glacier streams were running parallel to us.

After five hours of trekking, we took the pseudo lunch break. We put the mats on the ice, in fact, the porters did. Iqbal and few helpers had set up the mini kitchen right there on the glacier. We had the biscuit, green tea, and some dry fruits all while keeping our eyes on the K2. So far we had covered 4.34 miles and it had taken us five hours. After a thirty-five minute break, we were ready to leave. We were at 15,674 feet, and the high rise peaks surrounded us. K2 and its sister peaks, Broad Peak, Mitre Peak, G-IV, G-II and many others were overlooking us.

We kept marching, and the Vigne Glacier kept widening up; it looked like a giant ice slope. We were gaining altitude, and it was a consistently inclined slope. After one hour of marching, we took a slight right turn, jumped many streams, some flowing some frozen. We jumped over crevasses and took a sharp ascent to the Ali Camp. That significant increase in ascent had the drops on both sides to the crevasses which had gaps that we had to leap over. K2 was hidden from us now. As we ascended we could see a seasonal glacier lake on our right while leaving behind the vast land of ice on our backs. We could see the sun shining in the valley dominated by Vigne glacier below us. There was a range of straight, tall icy mountains, forming a long continuous wall of ice. We immediately named those mountains as "The Wall" as in Games of Thrones, and we assumed we were in the "wild" and we desperately need to cross the wall to go back to the "North."

At Ali Camp

At 2 p.m., we were at Ali Camp. Ali Camp was at sixteen thousand feet and approximately 6.35 miles from Concordia. We gained 1300 feet height since we had left Concordia. Ali Camp was a small area of boulders right next to a mountain; it was miraculously warm, relatively, of course. Something about its position made it a comfortable spot in this harsh rough territory. Other teams were present too, and since it was a small area, it felt crowded. Only kitchen tents were set up. There was no shade. At one side, there was an army check post overlooking the valley. The check post was nothing but a Pakistan flag pole and a green tent with two or three resident Jawans.

We rested in our kitchen tent. A young bearded guy peeped into our tent and introduced himself as Flight Lieutenant in the Pakistan Air Force. We invited him in to have lunch with us. He was the liaison officer with a Spanish team. He had been at the K2 Basecamp for months. He told us that due to the weather one of their advanced camp on K2 had been blown away by winds. Luckily, no climber was at the camp at the time of the storm. The expedition team had lost their expensive equipment worth few hundred thousand dollars at least but were content that there were no fatalities. Now, they have finished the expedition and concluded their season. They were going back via the Gondogoro La. Liaison officer's name was Abdullah as per him. He said that he was happy to see the many numbers of Pakistani trekkers.

We were to leave for Gondogoro La that same night, so rest was necessary. I couldn't rest that much because of anxiety. The stress of weather, the climb, the ropes, the duration, the descent, and lots of what if's were killing me. I then checked on my harness, headlamp, gaiters, and carabineer. I tested them and practiced putting them on and taking them off. Once you are out there, you are out there. Here is a piece of advice, always test your equipment before you would use them, always.

To Muneer Camp

I might had caught a nap of an hour or so, and it was already 9 p.m. We packed our bags and handed them to porters. We had our headlamps fixed on our heads and we layered ourselves up appropriately to climb in the cold. We put on gaiters, on our shoes. We stashed our harness and carabineer in our small backpacks.

By the time we started marching it was a quarter to 11 p.m. We were walking in single line. Our lead guide was Ali, and he was a quiet, serious young man. He was seasoned though and had been on this route many times, and he knew the path by heart and darkness didn't deter him.

We walked behind him in single file as scared kids. We were quiet, and we had no idea if we were walking on the edge of the cliff or were jumping over a crevasse, we were religiously following our guide step by step. We had already agreed on who would be the first and who would go last. We had to watch out for each other. Kashif was last, and I was second last, Kashif couldn't take the slow pace and paced up to be ahead of us. I objected and tried to stop him from breaking the agreed upon positioning, but it was fruitless. Kashif wanted us to reach early to beat the crowd for the ropes. I kept my position but was not feeling right about this out of safety concerns.

At Muneer Camp

In 45 minutes we were at the Munir Camp. We couldn't make out the place; it was just wide open space on snow, and we could see teams huddled together. One of the mysterious things that we noticed was a group of porters sitting around a fire and chanting prayers. It was so mystical and mysterious.

We saw a large group of people lined up and roped together. Shami then asked why we were not roped up? Was it too dangerous? And there must be reason others are roping up, why were we not? Shami asked repeatedly. Ali, our guide, tried to explain roping was not needed. Shami was not comfortable at all. Being a geek, he raised lots of what if questions and was going into a panic mode. What if he fell into crevasses, who would rescue him and how, were his repeated questions then. We tried to reason him, but he was freaking out. We tried to calm him down and told him if he stick close to the team then he would be alright. I said that whatever others were doing, in my opinion, did not make them safer in any way. You don't rope more than eight people in single rope and they were at least twenty people roped together in a single rope. That told me that they were amateurs. They were not trained to use ropes and that itself could kill them. Overall it was a disadvantage rather a safety. It took us while to calm Shami down.

After Shami's meltdown, we found out that Asim was not wearing gaiters. It would be another twenty minutes before he could get his gaiters on and in the meanwhile we enjoyed the freezing temperatures and the porters mystical chanting not so far away.

Figure 30: Top left: Concordia-Ali Camp trail; Top right & bottom left: Concordia-Ali Camp trail, Vigne Glacier; Bottom right: Porters and trekkers crossing ridge on Upper Boltoro Glacier after Concordia

Figure 31: Top left: Pseudo lunch break at Vigne Glacier, G-VII, G-V, and G-VI Peaks in the background (photo by Nouman K.); Top right: Trekkers on ascent to Ali Camp, Vigne Glacier and Vigne Peaks in the background (photo by Nouman K.); Bottom left & bottom right: Ali Camp and Vigne Peaks (photos by Salman Zakir)

13

DAY 9, TO GONDOGORO LA

La means pass in Balti language. The Gondogoro La, also known as GGLa, was our hope to cross the massive wall of Gondogoro Mountains. The GGLa ascent was to be done in the night when snow was hard. The hard snow made the steps more stable, and one could have good grip when snow would not be slushy. Night climb also meant that people ahead could leave good footprints behind that one could step on safely. It could also mean that it could be freezing and very dark long night.

When we started our assault, it was past midnight and pitch dark. It was all snow and there were no boulders. We couldn't make much sense of the terrain, but I bet it was beautiful. We had our headlamps on, and we marched on in a single line. We crossed lot of trekkers who had tied themselves to the ropes. They were using their rope, not the rope that was fixed in the route. The fixed rope was to come later.

It was all ascent, and we could feel the pressure on our thighs. We could only see what our headlamps would show us and white snow was all we could see. The porters were fast and they were crossing us in a hurry. Around 2 a.m., we were at seventeen thousand feet, and we were at the point where the fixed ropes started. We had to attach our harnesses carabiner to the ropes and start the steep climb. Some of us didn't have their harness on. We assembled and helped out the ones who didn't have the harness on them. The harness that Asim had purchased at the last minute turned out to be a medical harness that is used to move patients from bed to chair etc. It was not the mountaineering harness. It became a puzzle to us. Munna came along, and tried to figure out along with his helpers. We all chipped in for free advice and somehow stuck the harness on Asim's legs. Then Nouman K. needed help with his crampons. If the equipment had been checked before then, the entire team wouldn't have to freeze for one extra hour for the few unprepared.

The Rope Chaos

Once we were all ready, and all set, or so we believed, we hooked our harnesses onto the fixed rope with our carabiners. At the starting point, fixed rope was on the ground, and we had to bend down to hook ourselves. I was not sure why rope was needed at that stage. As we walked on the slope, it became sharp, and we were holding onto the rope to balance. I was sure there were steep drops on both sides. Most of us had not used the rope ever before for any climbing, so for the first thirty minutes, it was a total chaos. If someone put his entire weight on the rope or someone moved to the right or left without giving rope some slack then everybody latched to the rope swayed. A lot of us panicked. Some yelled at each other not to move, and some shouted to move.

I wish we had done some orientation before we tried anything like that. It was dark and cold, and we were hanging to the dear rope without much knowledge on what to do next. Because of our slowness and ineptitude to do anything a long line of people queued up. Climbers from the Spanish expedition team didn't tie to the rope and climbed parallel to the rope. They had ice axes and crampons and were well trained. For them, it was a climb in the park. Soon they rose high enough and were out of our sight.

It took me a good thirty minutes to grasp the situation and work out the strategy. I realized we could not sit on the slopes and freeze ourselves. We had to move and we had to move soon while making sure we were safe. I encouraged my team to take a step at a time and keep moving slowly. Finally, we started moving slow. I saw Shami holding onto the rope and sitting on the slope not moving. He was afraid to move. I stepped in front of him and asked him to take a step as I took a step. Shami was a quick learner, he noted my steps and my body position and followed. We all soon picked up the pace. Kashif had gone way up already, and I believed Nouman K. had gone up too.

This climb was something in which you were on your own. After a stretch of an approximately 800 feet climb, the rope ended. There was a small ledge where we were able to sit. We caught our breaths, we assembled and hooked ourselves to the next stretch of the rope which was hidden and buried under snow a few yards away. We had learned to climb using ropes, and we were getting better with each step. However we were also gaining height, and it was getting difficult to breathe which was getting us exhausted at faster pace.

The rope ended again and we took a break again. I saw Kashif waiting for us. He had a frightened look on his face. He told us that a porter ahead of him slipped and had dragged him down a few dozen yards before he could stop. The porter's luggage had fallen on Kashif and he was injured. I told Kashif to stick close from then on. By that time Asim was struggling too, and so was Nauman S. They were breathing heavy and were stopping after every step. I kept pushing them to keep moving. In my experience, taking long breaks after every step was not a good practice. One should continue even if one moves slowly. Eventually, one finds the rhythm. It was all about breathing. Your body becomes a machine and you need to find the ways to keep it operating.

The rope ended again but we found another stretch of rope. This had become a pattern and the rope became never ending loop. We were climbing and we were climbing one step at a time. All of a sudden it started snowing out of nowhere. The surroundings looked so surreal while we could only see the snowflakes in our headlamps light. Snowfall also meant that we would lose the footprints ahead of us.

We just kept climbing rope after rope. I was behind Asim, Nauman S., and I was worried about them, as they were showing signs of altitude sickness, especially Asim. In case something went wrong, I wanted to be with them to assist them or at least seek help if needed. Also if something happened to me, at least I had them around to assist me.

After a few more hours, the sun started to rise in the distance but it was still dark then. There was very low light but at least we were able to make sense of the terrain, and we could barely see the rope. At one of the ledges where we took some rest, a couple from the other team that just arrived were breathing heavily and were crawling on the ledge with pain and exhaustion. I recognized them because I had seen them before. I talked to them and helped them take off some layers of clothing on them. They were heavily packed and were sweating heavy. Sweat was not escaping their bodies. They were not getting much air. I spent ten to fifteen minutes with them. Eventually they seemed to recover a bit as their body could get more oxygen after taking some layers off. Imran, our helper, was with them and he had hooked the couple to his carabiner and was pulling them, sometimes literally. I urged them to keep moving as long as they were breathing.

I was moving slow and stuck close to Asim, Nauman S., and Shami for safety reasons. Others had sprinted and were ahead and somewhere up. We would not see them until we reached the top.

Gondogoro La Top

It had been five hours since we had latched to the ropes. By now we had stopped asking "are we there yet" questions. We were in our survival mode. As the sun was rising, and views were clearing up, we approached the summit of the pass. As we get closer to the summit, all the suffering turned to pleasure with every inch we gained. We were elevated, literally, and were ecstatic. Kashif, who reached earlier, was jumping with joy. It was festive moment for us. And to add to our delight, the views were amazing. We were close to nineteen thousand feet, and we could see K2 and all the eight-thousanders and seven-thousanders all around us. It was all magical. We were in the center of the thrones of mountains gods and for those few moments, we were the kings. There were some clouds but it seemed like they were pushed away by sun and wind.

There were no more ropes and we were at the top. The top was a slightly sloped flat area. We took selfies, pictures, and made some videos. There were peaks after peaks all around us. Our guide Imran and Iqbal urged us to leave this place as soon as possible. We had spent countless tiring hours to be here and they wanted us to leave right away. That was ridiculous, we thought. Those guys were not fooling around. They knew what was next to come for us, but we were ignorant. We were in the moment, and we didn't want to ruin it. As a celebration, Nauman S. and Asim tried to light a cigarette but they were put down by our guide, Imran. I had a hunch that if Imran was so serious then there must be something that we didn't know yet.

We may had spent twenty minutes at the top. At this height air was thin but the scenery was out of the world. Our efforts had paid off, and we were enjoying every moment of it. Our guides, Imran and Iqbal forcefully requested us to start our descent. "Sir, *idhar khatra hai, idhar log marta hai* (Sir there is danger here, people die here)." they said. I thought they were worried about the altitude. Nonetheless, we readied ourselves to descend the pass. We thought we were done with the most difficult part of the trek. The remaining would be a walk in the park for us. Oh boy, we were so wrong.

Gondogoro La Descent

There was some snow-covered flat plateau of a hundred feet we would cross before we could reach on the other side of the Gondogoro La, where the descent began. The views of this side were fantastic as well. There were peaks after peaks, though they were not like K2's side peaks level. Nonetheless, they too had a strong presence. The Laila Peak on that side did stand out, though, it was unique and a beautiful peak shaped like the slender pretty finger of a beautiful woman pointing to the sky.

As I walked toward the descent point, the snow disappeared all of a sudden. Seriously, at nineteen thousand feet altitude, we were back on boulders and small rocks. I saw a small crowd of porters sitting and watching. It did not give me a good vibe. It was windy and cold. What were they waiting on there for and why. When I closed in, I saw a sharp descent with a very narrow trek leading to the big rock where the rope was starting. The rope was thrown in the drop with some support of rocks a few yards further. I saw people clinging to that rope and moving slowly downwards facing the sky with their backs to the drops. There were not only extremely sharp drops on the sides but you actually had to reppel down one of the drops as well.

I thought this could not be real, that it was not fair. We had been through some tough climb and now this steep descent. This must be a big joke. That descent didn't seem to have an end. Now, the seriousness of the porters and helpers made sense. It was really too risky; one slip and you could be history.

I took deep breaths and moved forward toward the dangling rope. The only way to end this was to march on and cling to the rope. Munna was there at that start and signaled me to move ahead. "*Sahib, pathar aay ga, jaldi karo* (Sir, hurry up rocks will fall)."

It was a sharp descent with loose rocks. The snow would have helped, but there was none. I took deep breaths and lunged towards the rope with slow motion steps. A guy was guarding the rope, probably the same guy who had installed the ropes, was helping trekkers to latch on. I moved towards him like a scared goat. I was thirsty already. Bush was ahead of me in the line. Bush couldn't believe she came all the way from Manchester, UK for this creepy perilous descent. We had run into each other on the trek multiple times, and I could tell she was a good sport.

The rope guy latched Bush on the rope and signaled her to go. He then latched me to the rope and asked me to remain close to other trekkers to avoid an accidental rock fall. I saw Bush took calculated careful steps and then I saw her slip. She slipped bad and it was the rope that saved her. It was some while before she could gather enough strength and pull herself back up. It was my turn; I held the rope tight, took the step forward, and felt pressure on my feet, I was slipping, I put all my load on my shoulders to balance. But now my arms were hurting. I had to hold the rope tight to maintain grip, and it was draining energy. I was using my hands as brake pads against the rope. I was letting the rope go loose for a second which would make me free fall and then gripping it hard to stop the fall. It was not sustainable and I needed to transfer the effort to my legs to take the load. Nouman K. was right behind me. Nouman's shoes betrayed him and he slipped on every other step. He was totally exhausted after few falls.

Then all of a sudden, Nouman slipped and rolled toward me and fell on me. I had to use all my power to stop him from taking me further down. We both realized we were in deep danger. I asked him to step exactly where I had stepped. He would slip even where I stepped without any issue. He was in deep shit. I couldn't help much. I knew that, and so did he. He hollered to the rope guy and requested him to help him out. The rope guy came down and helped him with stepping and stayed with him. Nouman had professional help at his side so he would be okay.

After a few hundred feet down, I started feeling the burn on my hands, shoulders, and legs. I was thirsty as hell. I slipped on the rocks, and it was quite hard pulling myself up. After all, we were still close to nineteen thousand feet, and there was not much oxygen at that height for us.

The rope would sometimes sway left right without any advance notice. We would swing like a pendulum holding to the dear rope as tight as possible. The rope would usually swing if somebody down below slipped or someone just tried to drag rope to the side where one thought it should go. The rope was tight at spots when it was pulled tightly by others. At approximately nineteen thousand feet, descending via ropes with such swings, the views of the drops right in front of our eyes were haunting and daunting.

The rocks would frequently slip under our feet triggering frequent rock falls. The rocks fell towards me many times and at times it seemed that rocks were going to hit me, but then the rock would change its path. At times I was able to dodge the falling rocks. I was lucky.

The worst part was that I couldn't see an end to the slope and the rope. It was a very steep slope, and all I saw was never ending rope. My hands were bruised even though I had gloves on. My arms and shoulders muscles were tight, and my energy was dwindling. At certain points, the rope would end to start again at a different point. I would hug the rocks that deemed safe and attached myself to the next section of the rope. At some points rope had big knots, where I used one hand on the rope to hang tight and used my other hand to open a carabiner and locked it after the knot. The descent had become technical. I was doing the best I could, but I knew a lot was at stake. I was not alone and anyone could slip hard , swing, and take us down.

Kashif came behind Nouman K. and then Munna Ibrahim showed up behind Kashif. Finally, we were communicating and we were making progress. I knew if nobody had been looking, we would have cried. Asim caught up to us as well.

He was doing pretty good given that he was using a medical harness. We had spent three hours on the ropes and we were so done. We were hanging to our dear lives. We would make some progress and then would wait for blockage to clear away. I saw Bush slipped many times and at one stage she just laid there. It took her some time to gather some strength to get up. She was drained too.

Shami was stuck somewhere further up. We later found out that he had frozen in horror and wouldn't move. Other teams had to force him to sit aside and let others pass. Shami did make it, eventually, but it took him some time and lots of courage.

At last, after much prayers and swearing, the rope ended around seventeen and half thousand feet. My hands were dead tired and were bruised. All my muscles were aching terribly. I heard the sound of a big bang, thunders and then saw firsthand an avalanche falling on the mountain nearby. That sound and the slope was scaring the shit out of me. Did I tell you that a few years back, a guy had fallen from the same spot? He fell a thousand feet and had died on impact. He was a professional climber and was from Islamabad.

Munna, Kashif, Nouman, and I sat down to catch up on our breath and recover. Munna said that "It's all easy now." But what happened next was something that none of us had ever witnessed before.

The Accident

We then heard a scream followed by rocks falls and then heard continuous loud thumping sounds. What we saw next shocked us. We saw something roll up into the air and then hit the boulders and then it rolled into the air again and then hit the rocks again. It took us a few seconds to realize that something was actually somebody. Someone was falling and we were seeing this live as it was happening. That person, who had fallen, rolled into the air maybe three times and then pounded into the boulders same number of times before he took the final hit on the rocks. Finally, his body came to rest. At some distance, there was a steep drop and he could have easily disappeared into that fall for good, but he didn't. I thought he was lucky in that way, at least for now.

We were shocked and frozen; a few hundred of feet below somebody had fallen like a loose object, and now that person laid lifeless. We looked at each other in despair. He was way too down for us to rush toward him. Munna strongly urged us not to move at all. The guy must have slipped because of loose gravel and if we rushed we could slip as well. We were not out of danger yet.

We saw a few guys, who were at the same height as the fallen man, rushed towards him. We knew it was really hard for someone to be alive after such fall. We couldn't see any movement in the still body and we thought the person was gone for good. We knew it could easily be any one of us. The thought of our families rushed to our minds and that very moment all of us wanted to go back to our families right then.

Munna and Nouman jolted us back to reality and poked us to move. This place was a dangerous place to wait; a landslide or rock fall could happen anytime. We walked slowly and then crawled as if there was land mine somewhere and it would throw us into the air only to pound us back to the slopes. It was still rocky, but the slope was still very steep. My legs were literally shaking and I had lost all the confidence in my stepping.

As we moved down a little, we found a backpack, camera pack, and other belongings scattered around away from the narrow trail. These were the items of the person who had fallen. We cringed and moved forward. By this time we heard screams as if someone was wailing. Maybe a friend or his family member found out about the fall and was mourning and wailing. Our hearts sank. A trip for fantastic memories was becoming a trip for fateful memories. We were just served a reality check and it was a big one.

As I moved closer to the fallen guy, who by now was looked over by two people. I saw the man, who had fallen, up close. His skull was swollen and was red. His head had opened up. I couldn't muster the courage to go near him. I offered the guys my medical kit but they said they already had what they needed and thanked me. I asked if they thought he could survive. They shook their heads. They looked dismal and were not looked optimistic. I had run into these guys many times on the trail.

Suddenly fallen man started screaming repeatedly and would scream in terrible pain. I didn't know if those screams were of a dying man or a man with excruciating pain. All we could hear were his screams and someone saying "Hashim! Hashim!" probably to pacify him. We then knew his name. Hashim's screams were haunting us. I overheard someone saying that he had four hours to live. There was an American physician nearby and he rushed and did a quick check. He declared that given current conditions he needed medical assistance within next four hours or else there was no hope. Earlier on the descent, I had seen Hashim few yards below us on the ropes.

There was nothing we could do other than try to get some help, so we thought about moving on. However, we were so dumbstruck and paralyzed that we were finding it hard to cross a simple small glacier while navigating the steep slope we were on. Pyare Afzal was there too, he took charge of the situation and chartered us a route to cross that simple glacier. We noticed four other trekkers who looked somewhat trapped and were not able to move forward. Pyare Afzal cleared the backlog with diligence. Those four guys were on the same team as of the fallen person. Like us, those guys were quiet too. They followed us until we reached a safer terrain.

To Khushpang

We marched on with heavy hearts and legs toward the

Khuspang Campsite, our next stop. At around 17,000 feet terrain became relatively more reliable or rather it became more manageable. The scenery had been absolutely stunning all along. We were descending and we could see terrain thousands of feet below. There were glaciers and glaciated lakes in the valley floor and the valley had snow covered peaks on both sides. There was a green patch on the right side in distance. It was our destination, Khushpang. Khushpang means green grass in Balti language and that green grass was our campsite for that night. The terrain was still wild. Slopes were steep and path was narrow. There were boulders and sand on the trek. There was a hill on our right side and the steep drops to nowhere on our left side.

After what we had seen, we were walking slowly. Munna and other guides stayed behind as they wanted to check on rest of the team. We were alone on that trek and there was only one trek. There were large snow patches that we had to cross and then need to climb on the rocks and then go straight. It had been almost a straight twelve hours of continuous hard work and finally we saw some natural alpine like terrain. As soon as we reached the valley bed, a stream on our right side accompanied as all the way to Khushpang. We saw some green patches, some mountain flowers and mountain bees. We knew we were near Khushpang but it would take another hour to reach it. We crossed the stream and now the stream was on our left. There was one sharp ascent that we easily climbed and entered the Khushpang Campsite.

At Khushpang

At 15,000 feet altitude, Khushpang was a pleasant campsite on green grass with streams flowing on the left and one stream entering from the other valley on the right. Two valleys were merging here. Laila Peak, 20,000 feet (6096 meters), was the highlight of this site. There were two stone rooms next to the hill. They were serving as a seasonal canteen. There were two other small stone-walled rooms down below our tents with no roofs and no doors. The rooms had pits dug in the middle and were the toilets.

I easily recognized my mess tent and walked toward it. Munna was already there, and so was Nouman K. Bush was also chilling and recovering in our mess tent. Kashif was with me. Munna lunged forward and grabbed my feet and started untying my shoelaces. He said, "*Sahib*, you did good, you are our guest." I was moved by his gesture but I respectfully stopped him and told him that he was our guide and was very senior to us, and he deserved the big thanks, not us.

It was time to rest and relinquish, but my heart was still with the severely injured Hashim, who was probably still lying there in the open, screaming if alive. On my way to Khushpang I had come across some local people from the nearest village. They were carrying two large wooden poles and large red cloth piece. Information about the accident had spread like a fire, and these were the local volunteers who were heading to the accident area. They were fast walkers, and they were the only hope for poor Hashim. I cringed when I thought how they would put Hashim on the makeshift stretcher and how they would bring him down on such steep and treacherous terrain.

The nearest first aid was at the Hushe Village, and that was one more day of continuous trekking from Khushpang, and that's just basic first aid. I didn't think Hashim could even get first aid until the next night. He needed more than the first aid. He had struck his head hard on the boulders and I had seen his open red skull. How would he survive all this, I pondered?

Another thing that I pondered was that how come no team had a satellite phone. How come people with no training or at least some orientation were on such complicated and technical climb and descent. The weather was getting worse and Hashim had to be in Khushpang to be weather protected at least, assuming he was alive.

I recall that when I did Mount Shasta, which is approx

15,000 feet high snow-covered volcano in Northern California, with a couple of friends in 2005, we practiced the use of ice axes and crampons on side slopes before we actually attempted to climb. We tested our equipment and we would practice the techniques to how to effectively come to rest using ice axes if we fell on steep slopes. We did training hikes and climbs with different combinations. It was at least a month of training before we thought we were good to attempt Mt. Shasta summit.

I laid down and slept for an hour. Hunger and thirst awakened me. I hadn't eaten in a while. Our kitchen tent was not setup yet and I was in no mood to eat the biscuits. I walked up to one of the stone rooms. I asked a gentlemen in the chamber that if it was a canteen and if I could get some tea. He signaled me in. I went inside, and it was a cozy room. There were two goat skins on the floor, one white, one black. These were the rugs made of raw goat skin. It took me some time to adjust to the smell. The gentlemen in the canteen, an rugged face old man, was a local guy from the Hushe Village, who operated this seasonal bare minimum cafe. His son Imran was one of the helpers in our team. I knew Imran very well. After the tea, my hunger didn't ease. I asked him if there was something to eat. He cooked some fresh *roti* and heated up some leftover lentils. That was the best meal I ever had in a cozy mysterious stone room. I felt like I had time traveled few hundreds year back. I think, I paid him Rs 800 (8 USD) for the tea and *daal roti* (lentils with bread). He was not taking money, but I insisted; that was his living.

I was back in the tent after few hours and by that time all of our team had made it to Khushpang and everyone was discussing Hashim's fall. Shami knew Hashim and knew where he worked. Shami had become acquainted with him on the trek. Shami talked to Hashim's team lead and offered to make some phone calls to the people he thought could be helpful. A Spanish team had a satellite phone and they had offered to use the phone. Hashim's team lead was trying to call the Pakistan Army for a possible rescue. We knew that

Pakistan Army didn't do random rescue. You had to prepay for insurance for any possible rescue before you start your expedition.

Shami turned out to be an incredible support. He called his manager at Engro fertilizer and his manager then called someone and so on. After a few hours or so, Pakistan Army confirmed that there would be a helicopter rescue for tomorrow morning between 6 a.m. and 7 a.m., weather permitting. Shami worked in Engro fertilizer that was managed by Army and Hashim also worked in some company that was also managed by the Pakistan Army. So technically they were Pakistan Army's civilian employees so to speak. Shami was quick in his thinking and played the vital role of making connections. Kudos to Shami.

Some clouds came out of nowhere and blanketed the valley. It started raining hard and I didn't know how Hashim would be able to survive let alone make it to the Khushpang Campsite. Only in the morning, would we know the fate of Hashim. We were yet to see if Hashim could survive that night and yet to see if the helicopter could show up in this rough weather. His screams haunted me all night nonstop.

Figure 32: Top left: Gondogoro La at dawn. Top right: Trekkers heading out for Gondogoro La climb in the night; Bottom left: A guide taking break during Gondogoro La climb; Bottom Right: At Gondogoro La top, K2 and Broad Peak, partially covered by clouds, can be seen; (photos by Salman Zakir)

Figure 33: Top left: At Gondogoro La top, Laila Peak and its sister peaks can be seen in the background; Top right: K2 side peaks as seen from Gondogoro La top; Bottom: Trekkers at Gondogoro La top with K2 side views (photos by Salman Zakir)

14

DAY 10, THE RESCUE

It had rained heavy all night. I woke up around 6 a.m., and it was all quiet. The weather was bad, and I was not too hopeful if the rescue would or could happen. There was no helipad on the site. Time kept ticking away, and we paused all our activities in anticipation of the rescue. It was 7:30 a.m. and still no signs. We gave up hope. I was not sure if Hashim had survived the night. Why were things so quiet? I asked myself and curled up tight in my sleeping bag.

Then sky thundered with hard, I thought weather turned from worst to ugly. The sounds of thunder became constant and then I realized this could be the long-awaited helicopters, Hashim's ride back to life. We saw two Pakistan Army helicopters circling the Khushpang Campsite not too high above us. One helicopter landed on a tiny flat green patch right next to the stream. The other helicopter kept circling airborne. It was raining and it was too cloudy, yet they came and landed with authority. In next the few minutes, a group of people emerged from a nearby tent. They were carrying the injured on their stretched hands and arms. They all bowed their heads to avoid unforgiving helicopter's wings and loaded the passenger in the chopper. I didn't think there was any stretcher. It was all hand work. After few minutes, the helicopter was airborne and took Hashim and his backpack with it.

As the chopper went high up our hopes were lifted up too. Then helicopters disappeared down into the adjacent valley. We were still that high altitude. Hats off to the Pakistan Army rescue team to show up in such inclement weather and pull off a successful rescue. Later I ran into the same guy who was standing next to Hashim at the incident area. He told me that Hashim was lucky that his opened skull let the internal bleeding out. If the skull wouldn't have opened up then he may not had survived, he theorized.

Off to Saicho via Dalsampa

Once the helicopters left the Khushpang Campsite we all felt a weight lifted off of our shoulders. We started getting back to the daily grind. We had breakfast in our mess tent; no eggs this time. Eggs could not be carried across Gondogoro La. We still had some bread and honey etc. with tea and we were feeling great.

We left the Khushpang around 9:30 a.m. We started along the wide running stream but soon the stream disappeared and we found ourselves negotiating our way on the Gondogoro Glacier. It reminded me of the Vigne Glacier but miniature in scale; it still had some wild crevasses. A glacier stream was flowing through the glacier and would swing from left to right and then to the left. The stream would get narrow, then wide and then it would disappear and then roar back to the surface again. It was all clouds and fog. Thunderous cloud had calmed down but it was still raining light. We put on our rain jackets.

It was the first time we as a team were walking together. Munna Ibrahim, and Imran Nazeer, our guide, and helper, and then Saad, Asim, Kashif, Nouman K., Nauman S., Salman, Shami, and I were walking in a line. Shami was slow that day. I had observed that Shami started slow, but when he warms up, he somehow caught up and became unstoppable.

Shami had earned my respect for his role in yesterday's rescue. I was making my team wait up for him. This wait was upsetting to some. But it was better to be safe, even if someone was upset. Our shoes were making same ice crunching noise as we made while we crossed the Vigne Glacier near K2. The fog was lying low and it was mystical walking through the fog on a glacier while it rained on us. Asim asked how far Sampa Daal (Daal mean lentils in the Urdu language) was. We made fun of him because it was Dalsampa not Sampa Daal, and it seemed he was too hungry already.

Laila Peak and Masherbrum

Shortly, we passed the Laila Peak, 20,000 feet (6,096 meters). The Laila Peak was on our left. Laila Peak resembles a pointed slender finger of a beautiful lady. The word Laila is a synonym for a lovely woman whom one adores. Though its finger top was hiding in clouds, it still looked beautiful. Then we saw the Masherbrum, a 25,659 ft. (7,821 meters) high grand mountain, on our far right. It was the beautiful snowy mountain with a massive glacier spilled out from the top half of the mountain, which spread all the way to the Gondogoro Glacier down below. It would be a nightmare coming down through Masherbrum La. One of the teams we met in Urdukas a few days ago were attempting to do Masherbrum Pass, and we prayed for them. There were no clouds at Masherbrum, and we could see it loud and clear.

A glacier had a mysterious impact on my body. It's hard to describe, but my body acted weird when I walked through the glacier. It could be the ice, the crevasses, the slopes, the texture, then sun, exertion, altitude or the attitude. I didn't know what else. We had crossed 43 miles on Baltoro Glacier on foot, then a day on the Vigne Glacier, then Gondogoro La, and now this. I was tired of glaciers by now. Their beauty still amused me and I knew I would miss them as soon as I bid them farewell. But for now, I wanted out.

After about an hour after left the Laila Peak, we left the Khuspang glacier to our right and used the mountain ridge on our left to ascend the side mountain. Now we were out of the glacier. We were supposed to be relieved, but the trek became way narrower with steep climbs with steep drops to the same glacier we just left. Now we could see that the Khuspang glacier, which had become un crossable by foot, probably because the Masherbrum Glacier was merging that the Khuspang Glacier. There was one crevasse after another, with wide open dark mysterious gaps which were ready to swallow anything that comes its way. A portal to a cold world from which only a few lucky ones can get back.

Trek was mainly dirt trek by then and was green with sparse boulders. It would have been pleasant, but the steep drops to the glacier below gave us the chills. The track became trickier as it ascended steeply. We crossed a gushing stream that was falling into the Khuspang Glacier. The stream was on a steep slope and water was ravaging, Munna scouted the creek and found a safe crossing spot on the ascent. We crossed the stream, jumping through the rocks and balancing using our trekking poles.

Zoe Buffalo, Athletic, and Domesticated

We then noticed a yak-like animal on the trek trailing us. Imran Nazir, our guide cum helper, told us that animal was called zoe and it was a cross between black buffalo and a yak. Yak is a mountain Buffalo and is a rare beast. Local people have crossed yak with domestic buffalo and successfully came up with an athletic domesticated zoe. That buffalo zoe was up in the meadows somewhere and was going back to its shelter. Zoe was smart enough to follow the track and was an expert mountaineer. It crossed stream with careful stepping while observing the currents. We waited and let the zoe cross the stream and let it go ahead of us. Despite its enormous body and thin legs, it was faster than us, and we didn't want to run over by zoe's momentum. It was too intimidating at such a height on a narrow trek. Zoe's caretaker was far behind it, but that zoe didn't need any mending from anyone.

After the zoe crossed stream and us, we ascend again. We could see the valley filled with the unwelcoming vast glacier. There was an extreme descent facing drops to the glacier, and we took extreme caution. We crossed a dried up small stream and then climbed back up. Now, trackk disappeared, and we were to hug rocks hanging over the valley on our left side and jump from one rock to another without looking down. It was nerve wrecking. It was a long stretch, but it finally got over. I felt like a video game character of the game "Unchartered", in which character was supposed to jump from rock to rock while clinging to the mountain or wall with haunting drops under the feet.

Dalsampa, The Pole and The Bottle of Whisky

After that rocky stretch, we were back on the ridge with decent size trail on the left side. That ridge became a meadow, and that was our Dalsampa and Asim's Sampa Daal. It was the de facto base camp for Laila camp, but we found it deserted on our arrival. We saw a deserted stone structure far to our left. The rain had picked up, but we still decided to break for green tea and biscuits. It was well past noon. Everyone was tired, but all were in good spirits. We still had few more hours to go.

We had Maggie Noodles which we had hated, but in that rain it tasted way better than any five-star soup. Shami got hold of a Prince biscuit packet and consumed the entire packet like a cookie monster. Asim and Nauman S. took cigarette break even in the rain. Some things never change.

Masherbrum Peak, also known as K1, was on our right. The peak was not clearly visible, but we could see the Masherbrum La. The Gondogoro Glacier was not far below us. We saw a bottle of alcohol beverage, probably Whiskey, fixed on top of a pole in the rock pile in the middle of the

Gondogoro Glacier. We were curious what was that bottle of Whiskey doing there. Munna told us that there were three climbers from Portugal attempting to summit Laila Peak. One of the climbers fell into a crevasse and on knowing he wouldn't survive made his dying wish to erect a memorial for him with his favorite whiskey. It was an interesting way of being remembered. Mountaineers are always fascinating creatures.

When we left Dalsampa, it was all a slow but continuous descent onwards. The glacier turned into full flow stream on the rocks. We would walk through the dried up creek bed while brown colored stream flowed next to us ignoring our existence. It was still raining light showers. All the peaks looked mystical because of the fog created by the clouds. The sun had started to make its way into the valley, and it looked magical.

The stream took a slight left turn at some point, and we began moving to the right with a ridge between us and the stream. We were walking in the valley now. We were walking on the grass track marked with stones on both sides. We knew we were near some settlement but it was not the case. The valley ended and we started descending on the rocky path again. The stream came back into view and was far below on our right side. It was a rocky trail, but it was manageable, and the drops were not that dangerous. The path was wide enough for us to walk comfortably. Then we found ourselves walking through scattered trees. The trail was more domesticated with continuous stone laid on both sides. After thirty minutes, we were walking into the Saicho Campsite.

Saicho Campsite and Another Bakra Night

It was 4:30 p.m. and we were at about 11,600 feet altitude. The clay path had lead us into the campsite. We could see many valleys confluence at this area. This campsite was a fairy tale campsite. It had running smooth streams, decent tree spread, turf was all flat, and green grass all over. There were signposts to K6 and K7 peaks. K6 and K7 peaks were visible in some distant. One needed to hike to have better views of the K6 and K7. There was a reasonable sized canteen with chairs and tables. It had been awhile since we had sat on chairs, so we grabbed the chairs and sat on them as if there was no tomorrow. How many things in our lives we take for granted. I never thought chairs were such a luxury. We had green tea and cracked jokes. Shami grabbed the Prince biscuits packet and became the cookie monster again. Nauman S.' lips had swollen due to allergies and we were picking on him. We told him that his wife would not let him in the house. His lips were so swollen that he could kiss his one-year-old son in Lahore from here. We all had fun at the expense of his misery. We did give him Vaseline and anti-allergies medicines, which helped recover his lips but not his pride.

In this fairy tale campsite, a cool donkey was minding its grass near a smooth running stream. That donkey also looked so fairytale like. It reminded me of Shrek's donkey as in the Shrek animated movies. That donkey remained at the same spot for the entire day.

This day was another scheduled *bakra* (male goat) night. As a thanks to our porters, we as a group, were to treat the porters with the goat. A goat, which they would happily slaughter, skin, and barbecue. We would get some post thanks leftovers later so we waited in anticipation. We napped in our tents for some time. Around 8 p.m., we were summoned to a raised concrete rock structure with high roofs. There were two rooms and a gallery. Our cooks and helper had running coals on a grill on which they were barbecuing goat steak cuts. The rooms were filled with barbecue smoke. We sat on the floor with local people, mostly porters, and guides from different teams.

Only our team was invited to join them. There were many Balti people in the room, and I could tell from their conversation they took pride in their hospitality and loved their mountains. They were talking in Balti language but would turn to the Urdu language to fill us in. They had rich traditions and culture, but they didn't have universities. They were hardworking people. They start as a porter, work up the chain to become lead porter, and then cook, and then a guide. If they become good at being the head guide, they are sought out by international expeditions. If they become good at being a porter, they can become high altitude porters. High altitude porters are the backbone for any summit team, and they are the one who fix ropes at higher elevations and carry provisions between high camps and lower camps. They are the lifeline of any expedition. They could cost around $1,000 per day, and good ones are hard to find. They are the ones who regularly put their lives at risk. If there were training centers for mountaineering, then it could provide a boost to the local economy and pride. For now the lucky and hardworking ones got trained on the job, only if they land on the right job at the right time. Porters were hardworking mountain people, but they were not mountaineers. They had the good training grounds and the right altitude, all they needed was the right attitude.

Between the delicious barbecue and Pepsi, yes a Pepsi, we had great discussions. We were jealous of their rich culture and rich environment and they were envious of the opportunities we had. We had access to good education in our cities in Punjab and thus most of us were either engineers or entrepreneurs and regardless of our own shortcomings we were the rich people for them.

One More Round of "Jhoot Pay Jhoot" (Lie After Lie)

Playing cards was our favorite past time whenever we had the energy and time to indulge. Most of the time we would like to take rest to recover, or we would only sit out and stare out the beauty around us.

When it came to playing cards, we would play a game called the "bluff", the most common game known to us all. Bluff was a card game in which your goal was to get rid of your cards by bluffing. You would throw the card in pairs and announce the card types. If you didn't lie about your cards then who ever checked your cards would have to pick them up. Whoever got rid of their cards faster would be victorious. Munna Ibrahim had joined us in many games before, and he had been pure fun. He would shake his head often and called us the people who would lie after lie (*jhoot pe jhoot*). Thus Bluff game was called *jhoot pe jhoot* since then onwards. Let's have *jhoot pe jhoot* was our calling.

Imran Nazir, our beloved cook cum guide, also joined us in our shared mess tent. An innocent looking Balti, Imran turned out to be a professional and kicked our asses in Jhoot Pe Jhoot. Next day we were supposed to be in Hushe which was a proper village so we knew this might be our last night in the wilderness. We were happy and sad at the same time. We took to our sleeping bags very late that night.

Figure 34: Top left: Gondogoro La descent using ropes; Top right: Trail leading to Khushpang Campsite after Gondogoro La descent; Bottom: Helicopter rescue in progress at Khushpang Campsite (photo by Salman Zakir)

Figure 35: Top left: Team walking in single profile to Saicho Campsite; Top right: Saicho Campsite; Bottom: Hushe's welcome gang; (photos by Salman Zakir)

15

DAY 11, OFF TO HUSHE

We woke up easily into that fairy tale morning around 7 a.m. The birds chirping, the stream whispering, and the smooth clean air blowing. It was sunny and bright. That fairytale donkey by the stream was gone. At 8 a.m., we were summoned to the same raised structure where we had dinner last night.

Our breakfast, to our surprise were special local *parathas*. They were different than *parathas* in the Punjab. These were crisp and were made from the locally grown wheat. We didn't stop eating until we got tired. They were so delicious, and our appetites had opened up at that altitude as well. I still recall the look that cooks had when they had to keep cooking for our insatiable appetite.

We packed up around 9 a.m. and were ready to leave. Salman, our Sallu Bhai, had lost his sunglasses and claimed that somebody had taken his glasses. When the campsite gets crowded, your things could disappear easily. It was not a good day for Salman, as it was a bright sunny day and there were approximately six miles of trekking that day. So glasses were badly needed.

After some complaining, we were on the trek. The very first thing we crossed was a gushing full stream coming from the K6/K7 side. There were three wooden planks nailed together and put on a raised platform on each side. The raised platform was the bridge. We felt spoiled. Nonetheless, it made our heads spin when we crossed it.

Now, we had brown mountains dominating the valley. Snowy white mountains were on our backs and were getting further behind. Trek was wide and it had stones on both sides to mark the trek, but no boulders on the trek itself. It was a smooth trek the majority of the time and there was a slow descent. After an hour's hike, we started seeing small empty structures that were meant to store livestock to safeguard them against inclement weather. The valley was wide with Shayok River flowing in the center. There were green patches high up on the brown mountains where, as per Munna, markhor could be seen. Markhor is the rare wild goat found at the highest altitude. Markhor is fond of green grass on steep hills on inaccessible areas. The snow leopards are also known to be found in these areas, and these shy creatures are fond of markhor. Only the snow leopard can hunt markhor on such sharp cliffs. If we want to see snow leopard then, winter would be the best season. In the winter, these rare cats had to come down to hunt.

Today was the day for Nouman K. to get upset. After witnessing the accident first hand, we all had a strong desire to call home and let our families know that we were safe and to check in on our families. Munna had told us that after Saicho there would be some spots where he could get signals on his phone. Though we all had phones Munna had a phone with the local network that worked mainly in Baltistan region. And of course, that local phone network was random and sparse due to the terrain and remoteness. Unfortunately, we couldn't get any signal around the area where Munna had promised. Nouman hiked on extra amount of time to look for the signals but with no luck. He was visibly upset and didn't talk to any of us, let alone Munna. Nouman felt that

Munna played him. Nouman marched on ahead of us with large mad steps and disappeared. We didn't see him until later that night. We felt Nouman's pain and Munna's helplessness, but we couldn't do much, and we marched on.

Hushe's Welcome Gang

After one more hour of hiking, we ran into a gang of eight to ten cute kids, aged between eight to twelve, I presumed. They were the first other people we had seen in almost two weeks. The roaming kids were a clear sign of a village nearby which that made us ecstatic. The kids were welcoming and each of them shook hands with each of us. I had a trail mix in my backpack. I had bought this trail mix bag from the US with me. It had dried fruits, nuts, cashews, and M&Ms. I gave away my trail mix to the kids who had encircled me. They wiped cleaned the trail mix bag in few microseconds. Such are small but real pleasures of life.

Those kids then tagged along with us for the next hour, all the way to Hushe village. They were talkative and would tell us about things. They were on a summer break. They sang their ABC to show that they know their stuff. They were all in *shalwar qamees*, somewhat worn out. They were wearing sweaters, jackets, sandals, and slippers, all in sheer contrast with their youthfulness. Some were wearing colorful beanies. They had thick dark brown hair; thick mainly due to the untidiness. You could tell they spent the entire day out in the open valley. One of them introduced himself as Rohullah and then introduced his fellow buddies as Kashif Ali, Fida Ali, Ghulam Ali, Sana Ali, Abdullah, and Moin Khan. We became good friends for the next hour.

A short while later we hit a wall the trek was blocked by a large stone wall. Our little guides showed us the way to a ladder that would let us to the other side. Stones were put together to build a wall to keep the livestock out in the green pastures. It was to make sure that their animal didn't wander off that far. After one more hour of the hike, we were walking through many small empty stone walled structures and then the long grass fields. We then saw two story concrete and stone structure with a silver tin roof on a hilltop at a distance and hoped that that was our destination for that day. We hiked up to that building, and I couldn't help but notice the plastic bags and plastic wrappers that were scattered around the hill. Trash was a clear sign of a settlement. Where there are people there will be trash.

Refugio Hushe Hotel

That two-story building that we saw in distance was Refugio Hushe Hotel, our camping site for that night. It was established by a Spanish non-profit and all the earnings from the hotel were given back to the Hushe community. Spanish management lived in the hotel to oversee the operations. The first floor had a lobby and dining hall. The second floor had ten rooms available for rent. Each room was named after a peak. So you could either stay in a K2 Room or a Nanga Parbat Room for example. There was a large front porch which had five jeeps parked, probably for our ride back to Skardu. We rested in lobby. We were officially in Hushe.

Nouman K. was still nowhere to be found. The last we heard was that he was seen at a small tuck shop buying candies for the local kids and looking for phone service. Hushe was Munna's and many other porters' hometown. I gifted my Old Spice body spray to Munna as I had promised him on the trek. A happy Munna then disappeared for an hour or so and showed up smelling fresh. Saad and I reminded Munna of his promise for a phone call.

Hushe Village and Hunt for Cell Phone Signals

Munna took us for the hunt for cell phone signals in his village. He had his small mobile phone in his hand, and we walked around. The village had three to five streets that merge back to each other. If you walk around, then you could reach the end of the village in maximum of ten minutes. Streets were all clay street with small, open drain trench running alongside it for the most part. You could see some shops selling necessities, but nothing fancy. Houses were made using local wooden poles, and local stones glued together with mud. Some houses were cement plastered and were lightly whitewashed. But the majority houses were built using simple rocks and sticks. Houses had a common pattern. All the houses were low roof with a square open hatch in the middle of the roof. These mud roofs were flat and were used as a platform to sun-dry apricots and other food items during summer.

In winter, low roofs helped kept houses warm with less wood consumption and roof hatch worked as exhaust. All houses had a room for wood stock and room to store livestock. Livestock could not survive the winter out in the open. There were also some signs of modern life. One could see few electric poles and a transformer. Few select houses had satellite dishes on their roofs, too. We spotted a tractor, a few motorcycles, and a pickup truck.

One of the prominent and well-built structures was the central mosque. It was a huge two-story structure with a wooden framework filled-in by light gray stone walls. There was some paintwork on the wood embedded in stone walls, giving the impression that many ladders were going up to mosque roof. In between, there were painted windows of yellowish-olive color. On the ceiling there was a wooden green block structure and a golden spike, acting as a minaret and a symbol of Hushe's religious ethnicity. Woods were painted maroon, and gave a nice contrast with gray stone walls. That day the mosque was active due to the Friday sermon and prayers.

Greg's CAI

We saw two school buildings which was as very pleasant

and welcome surprise. The non-profit Central Asia Institute operated one of the schools. Central Asia Institute (CAI) was founded by Greg Mortenson, the author of New York best seller book "Three Cups of Tea". In 1993, Greg was with a K2 expedition but got separated from his team. He was rescued by people of Khorpe Village, near Askole. He was then provided shelter and refuge by Khorpe people. Greg was so impressed by the hospitality and so moved by the poor conditions of the people that he decided to do something for them. The Khorpe villagers asked him to help build a school if he could.

Greg, originally from Montana, U.S., was motivated to keep his promise. He kept his promise and helped build a school in Khorpe within next three years. He then started a non-profit called CAI and started building schools in similar remote areas. But recently the CAI had been under scrutiny over misuse of funds and had been criticized especially in the US. Out of curiosity, I asked Munna how CAI had been doing in their area and if there was any foul play? He said there were no complaints there and the CAI had been doing a great job and had a positive impact on the community. Somebody must have taken advantage of CAI, but overall they had been a great help.

In Hushe, everybody knew everybody. Munna especially was known to all. Wherever we went, people came up to Munna to greet him. Since Saad and I were with him, we were considered his guests and we were greeted with warmth as well. The atmosphere gave us feelings like we were in a large family compound. Even women would come up and greet Munna, and they would shake hands and would exchange pleasantries. All of them were cousins or related somehow. Women were either sitting out in the streets next to their doors or were carrying cones like baskets to transport little kids or the goods. Kids were on their own. I didn't see anyone worrying about their children. When we asked Munna where his children were, he said they would be here somewhere. We then joked that all the kids were his. He cracked open with laughter.

Munna's House

Munna led us to his home. It was Saad with him and me at that time. We entered through the small brown door, bypassed a empty livestock room, took some steps up, and crossed a tiny courtyard with an open hatch roof. There were two rooms in total. We could see his curious family, his wife and a young girl and a little boy staring at us. Munna lead us to the other room. It was a small room with wide windows with views of the valley below. There was a small bed on one side and rest of the room was covered with thin red carpet. A mattress was welcoming us with round pillows fixed alongside the walls. There was also a small mattress on the side with pillows. There were family pictures on a shelf above the window. Our heads could touch the roof and roof had round wooden poles spanning the width of the room. We were like kids who had somehow entered the cute home in a fantasy town.

There was another tinier room attached to this room. That room had a timeworn washing machine, probably used as storage, few loose wires running overhead, an Indian commode, and a large blue bucket. Munna heated up the water for us. Saad and I took turns showering in this tiny room in a tiny house in far far away village of Hushe. Munna's wife made us tea. His hospitality moved us. We said hi to his cute family. Munna had a landline phone in his house and that had no connection either. Surprisingly, we noticed a small television in the room and it was playing footage of some political event happening in my home city of Multan. How technology can connect people and possibly corrupt their simple lives.

I had noticed that there were no glass windows in Hushe houses. Probably, they needed a square opening in the middle of their houses for the sunlight. All windows were wooden, and painted the same color. Due to weather, they needed to keep their wooden windows closed majority of the time.

Cell Phone Connection Finally! Random Stroll

The shower had given us new life and we went back to the hotel cum camping site. Shami, Kashif, I took Afzal with us this time to look for cell phone signals. We walked around and finally found the spot where there was signal. It was the same spot that Munna had brought us to earlier, but since everything runs on a generator, the transmitters might have been shut down when we tried earlier. Still, it was not that easy. The cellphone had to be positioned at a certain angle and at a certain height to establish the connection. After multiple attempts, we were able to make calls to our loved ones, one by one. I dialed my U.S. number and my heart beat increased as I heard the voice of my wife at the other end. It was 2 a.m. in the U.S. and she was worried at first. I checked on our kids and I told her I was okay. It was hardly a two minutes call but it meant a lot to me. I didn't want to consume all the minutes of Afzal's phone.

As we walked randomly through random streets in the Hushe Village, we saw a lot of cute kids, from all ages, one to twelve years. They would approach us and would say "Hello, chocolate please." Unfortunately, we were out of chocolate by then, but when we would say "How are you?" in Urdu then they would act little surprised. Looking at the number of kids playing around, I wouldn't be surprised if Hushe would transform from a village to a big town in just 20 years from now.

Munna stopped a young kid passing by and hugged him, talked a little, and then let him go. Munna turned around and told us that this kid's dad was killed in an attack at Nanga Parbat Basecamp in 2013. It was a brutal attack and a massacre by terrorists that claimed eight innocent foreign mountaineer's lives and that kid's dad's life. Munna, with some grief in his voice, said that the group had been his. We felt for him and before we could inquire more he changed the subject. I guess he didn't want to talk about that tragedy. We had seen him hurting after Hashim's fall and now we were trying to remind him the massacre of nine people of his group. We respected his privacy and moved along with him on Hushe streets.

Friday Prayers and the Mourning

Shami and I went to the mosque for the Friday prayers. We had missed Friday group prayer but we did pray on our own since it had been so long since we had last offered our prayers. The mosque was built on a raised stone structure. It had three rows of wooden pillars in its main hall. Each row had four pillars and each pillar must be thirty feet tall at least. The pillars were all beautifully crafted. The roof had a good stylish pattern made of wooden planks. On the left and the right side of the hall and slightly above, there were crafty balconies. The balconies had beautiful woodwork done and were painted a shade of yellow. In the middle of the hall, there was a simple but elegant large, white, ten bulb chandelier, and to its left, there was a large lantern hanging from a rooftop as well. The chandelier looked great, but I guess lantern was far more effective than the fancy chandelier.

Right, when we were finishing our prayers, people started gathering in the mosque and men starting forming one big circle. Women also began to come to the hall. They would sit in the back a little farther from the men. Their young kids would put some kind of homemade bread in the middle of the men's circle. Soon a man within that big circle started reciting some poems in the Balti language. He had pain in his voice and slowly people began mourning in a semi loud weeping noise.

They were mourning the death of grandsons of the Prophet Muhammad (S.A.W), Imam Hasan and Hussain (R.A), who were mercilessly slaughtered along with their families in the city of Karbala in Iraq some 1400 years ago.

They were denied their claim on the caliphate and a powerful tribe who had a counterclaim, mercilessly massacred Hasan and Hussein along with their families and followers. All devout Shiite Muslims have mourned the deaths of Imam Hasan and Hussein every year since centuries. We slowly and humbly backed out of the mosque. We didn't want to interfere with their religious gathering.

Porters Closing

We returned to the hotel lobby. Shami's cellphone charger was gone again, and he was visibly upset about his charger disappearance. Shami asked the lead porter, Wali, if he or any of his porters had seen a charger. Wali took this question as an accusation and responded with some heat. That simple question "Have you seen it?" turned into a mini brawl in few minutes. Some of us interfered and pacified both parties. It was our first day in civilization, and we were already at home.

That day was the last day for all the porters, and their payments were being finalized. As per Munna, one should always watch out for their items more carefully at two times: the first night and the last night of camping. The first night and the last nights are most popular days for items going missing. At the first night, porters who couldn't secure a contract might pick up things out of desperation. At the last night, porters might pick up items taking comfort in the fact that they wouldn't be seeing the group anymore after that night. Also, onlookers and other team members could become little greedy.

We among ourselves decided to tip the porters. We as a team decided on a fair amount and pooled in money for porter's tip. I pulled Munna aside and gave him additional five thousand rupees for him and his team. That was almost all I had at that time. I did keep some change for my emergency needs, though.

Little Karim

While we were going in and out of the Refugio Hotel lobby, Asim pointed out to guy sitting at the reception desk and said: "Look, he is Little Karim." The guy must have been in his mid 60s. He was short in height for sure but his legendary stories still echo from the Karakoram to all the way to the Europe. He was wearing a white woolen cap with round edges and was dressed in a high-quality breathable jacket of brand "Acertryx" over his dark gray *shalwar qamees*. He had some taste. I had heard a lot about him and felt minuscule in front of him.

Nouman K. and Asim were his biggest fans among us and somehow opened the conversation with Little Karim. Little Karim, now retired, was a passionate mountaineer with a track record of great successes. He graciously agreed to spend some time with us. We went out and sat on the campsite grass ground and circled around him. We had fantastic views of Hushe Valley and we savored both the views and Little Karim's company.

Little Karim's real name was Abdul Karim. He was born and raised in Hushe. His family was a given communal pasture area near Gondogoro peaks to shepherd their livestock. As a kid, he would spend most of his time at his family allotted pastures and would climb the tricky rocks at a very early age. He had always loved climbing even though his family would try to stop him for his safety sake. Gondogoro was not known to outside mountaineers, and thus there was no traffic of adventurers moving through Hushe or Gondogoro area of any kind whatsoever.

One day, to Karim's surprise, a team of foreigners descended into his family's pastures through Gondogoro. Little Karim was a very young kid and still remembered the candies and biscuits that team shared with him. Excitedly, Little Karim showed off the biscuits to his mother but his mother was little suspicious because she hadn't seen anything like a biscuit in her life before. Little Karim knew then that if somehow he could become part of such expeditions then he could have lots of biscuits. That love of climbing and love of biscuits would then set the course for his life.

When Karim became of age to work as a porter, he was denied entry to any expedition because of his short height and kid-like features. He persevered and made to a team as an entry level porter and progressed through the ranks like he would climb the rocks.

It was not only his skills that distinguished him from others but also his empathy and compassion to help others. Once he had jumped into the Baltoro river to save a British mountaineer who had fallen into the river. He rescued many trapped climbers by quickly reaching them with life-saving supplies in the worst of the worst weathers. He had in some instances single-handedly carried down climbers to safety. He had famously single-handedly hauled supply of 25 kilos to the high altitude advanced camp to help to a flailing team just in time. There had been some cases that he had fallen into a crevasse but had been lucky enough to come out of them alive and on time. Perhaps saving others had invisibly given him an extended lifeline.

He became a highly sought after high altitude porter and became a lifeline for the expeditions to Karakoram peaks. He was considered a match for the high altitude porters of Nepalese Sherpas. The French had been so impressed by Karim that they had made two documentaries on him, "Little Karim" in 1985 and "Master Karim" in 1997. These documentaries had made him a sought after celebrity in France. Little Karim was then called on to be a judge on film festivals in France. He would make appearances at many forums and would conduct workshops for the French enthusiasts. Little Karim of Hushe was not so little after all in France.

He was invited to settle in many countries, but he had politely declined. "I love my village, I love Islam, Pakistan is Islam for me, and I am not leaving Islam and Pakistan" that's what he told us. I may say so, in my opinion Karim played a pivotal role in building confidence for foreign expeditions to rely on local resources which are now considered at par with any international resources for high altitude missions.

Little Karim Manzil

We couldn't believe our luck when Little Karim asked us if we would care to see his albums and awards and join him for tea at his house. He asked us to be at his house late afternoon. We said yes, of course.

Karim's modest house was near the Refugio Hotel's campsite where we were stationed. Karim's house was on a raised stone foundation and we had to take four steps up to reach to his door. At the top of the door, there was nailed frame that said in first line "Bismillah Rehman Rahim (In the name of Allah the most merciful and gracious)," in Arabic and the second line said, "Hajji Abdul Karim Little Manzil." in Urdu. There was a white fluorescent bulb fixed on top of that irregularly shaped wooden frame.

Like other houses in Hushe, the entrance was very humble. We entered into a small courtyard with the roof of irregular shaped wood pillars held together by rough wooden planks. There was a square opening in the middle that would provide sunlight and access to the roof. We could see various sized blue canisters on the side along with large utensils. Everything here was about storage and survival against harsh winters. We could see the kitchen ahead of us with the bare minimum utensils and a wood stove in the middle. We went toward the room to our left, removed our shoes, and entered the room. It was somewhat dark by now and the only fluorescent light bulb in the chamber would flicker continuously.

One wall showcased his pictures and magazines cutouts that were now his prized possessions. We could see a French magazine's cut out portraying him in his prime advertising documentaries made about him. He had been a handsome, smiley man with tons of confidence. Those pictures were a definite statement of his accomplishments. We went through his albums and then the magazines in which he was featured. They were mostly European magazines. We enjoyed his albums in which he was a judge in a film festival in France. Some of the pictures that struck me were the ones where there were teams of French people, young and old, girls and boys, listening to what Little Karim from remote Hushe village of Pakistan had to say. I wish our people had done that as well.

Little Karim's wife burned some wood, which was probably collected from nearby woods, under the kitchen stove and then boiled water, which was probably laboriously fetched from a nearby stream. She then made us green tea. That little house was then filled with the smoke of burning wood for a little while. We were moved by their efforts. They were trying to make sure we, their guests, were comfortable. Munna who happened to be Karim's cousin pointed to a black and white picture of little kids. He pointed at one of the kids and asked us to guess who was that little fellow. Before we said something, he said that that was him, Munna Ibrahim, with his cousins. Munna was beaming with pride.

We settled down on the floor mattresses with our backs to the wall and let the great Little Karim talk. Little Karim, overwhelmed with our attention, shared his interesting stories slowly but steadily.

From Abdul Karim to Little Karim

He said that by 1979, he had been a high altitude porter for some time. He was with the French expedition at that time. It was a big French government sponsored expedition. There were three porters named Karim. Whenever the *gora* (white guy) would ask for Karim, all three Karims would respond. One Karim was a big fat fellow from Khaplu Village, one Karim was from Shigar Valley, and he was the one from Hushe Village. At that time they didn't know Urdu language. They only knew the Balti language, so it was all sign language that was used to communicate. The *gora* then finally said if he said, Big Karim, then the Karim from Khaplu should come and if he called Medium Karim then Karim from Shigar should respond and if he said Little Karim then Karim from Hushe should come. Since then he was known as "Little Karim."

How Little Karim Become Famous

Little Karim said that one of the reasons that he became famous was that he was fast at climbing. He said his feet moved automatically, moving fast was part of him, and he didn't have to think about it. Other reasons were that he had carried 25 kilos to high altitudes at faster than expected speed which helped saved many lives at high altitudes.

Climbing Then and Now

He said Polish climbers were really good. One of them did the "magic line" in 1986. The "magic line" also called the suicidal route and was the toughest route to climb the K2. So far only a Spanish climber was able to summit the K2 via "magic line route" in 1996.

He turned out to be not a big fan of Messner, the mountaineering legend. As per Little Karim, Messner was a great climber, although he was a little arrogant. He would only keep to big guys. Messner was only polite with big guys. Messner would discourage people who would like to meet him or have a photo with him. He said that during his time's climbers were really good. They were good natured as well. These days climbers are not that great. English are the worst now, they fight. Before, they were nice. He thought that because there were no roads, teams had to spend five to six months in these areas, so they mingled more.

Karim had lived at K2 base camp for four months. In 1983 he climbed K2 from West Route. Karim had climbed

K2 three times. Two times he went up more than 8,000 meters. Once he was 200 meters short of the K2 summit, but unfortunately, the weather got worse, and he stayed two days at Camp-V on K2 before he returned. On one of the attempts in 1998, a British climber with him had died during the climb. There used to be only five to six expeditions per year. There was no road to Dassu, a town way before Askole. It would take fifteen to eighteen days to reach K2 Basecamp. Only the serious people would come back then. Their equipment was heavy and he had never liked the big crampons for climbing. For Little Karim, crampons were a safety hazard because they could entangle climbers and cause a fall.

Before we said our good byes, I asked him if he had ever been afraid for his life. He stated that he had never been afraid because he always had faith. If he ever had let fears control his life then he could have never climbed. Mountain climbing was nothing but conquering your fear. We took some pictures with him and took our leave. It was time well spent and it was one of the highlights of our trip.

Closing Night at Hushe

We were back in the Refugio Hotel lobby by 8 p.m. or so. Our tents were pitched outside, but we were enjoying the sofas and some basic modern amenities such as electric lights in the hotel lobby. We had a delicious dinner of *aloo anday* (egg curry), chicken curry, rice, French fries, *roti* along with a Pepsi. To our pleasant surprise, we were served custard as a sweet dish. It was such a treat. A policeman showed up, his name was Ishaq. He was friendly and he wanted to check if everything was okay at our side. That was so unlike police that we were used to in Pakistan. He had one official piece of business, though. He was supposed to compile a list of people in the group. He was there to tally the list that was compiled at the Dassu check post that we crossed before we started trekking. The list was for the safety of the travelers through the region. He was very pleasant and he told us that there was zero crime in the area and only issues people had were regarding land disputes.

I don't recall what time we went to our tents. Before we hit the sleeping bags, we had a discussion of what do with the day that we had skipped at Concordia. Some suggested that we should spend an extra night in Khaplu, or probably in Skardu. There was even a discussion of spending one more night at Hushe. But deep down, we all wanted to be back at our homes as soon as possible. Overall, we were content and had a great sleep as soon as we were in our sleeping bags. We knew we were almost home.

Figure 36: Top left: Little Karim's wall of fame in his house; Top right: Little Karim telling his life stories at his home; Bottom: The team listening to Little Karim in Refugio Hotel back yard; (photos by Nouman K.)

16

TO SKARDU VIA KHAPLU

It was a relaxed morning. Trekking was over, and now our goal was to get back to Skardu that day. Around 8 a.m., we compressed ourselves into an elongated Jeep. Ten of us were in the jeep and our luggage was on the jeep's roof top. Saad decided to hang out of the jeep window to enjoy the fresh air and avoid uncomfortable closeness with other fellows. We started the ride in good spirits. It was a narrow dirt track through the village and then open fields and then it was just the jeep track, the mountain, and the river. There were some sharp switchbacks on which the jeep required reversing into the mountain to negotiate the turns. The jeep crossed a wooden hanging bridge that would sway as the jeep moved through it. After half an hour there was another wooden bridge, but this time it was higher and longer. The river was large and was way below us. The hanging bridge had loose wooden planks and we prayed those planks held together while we passed through them.

Trout Farm

Right before Khaplu, the driver pulled the jeep into a trout fish farm. It was a pleasant fish farm on the foothills of the mountain. It had two pools for trout and local fish. We ordered trout and volunteered to catch the trout ourselves. Shami had been bugging for fishing since we started the trip. It was his chance to do some fishing though in some controlled environment. We used wooden sticks and used bread to entice the trout. We turned out to be true amateurs in fishing and the farm staff pitched in to save us from further humiliation and possible starvation. The fish was fresh but since it was farmed fish it tasted like wheat to me. It turned out that these fish were fed wheat most of the time. Fish in fresh water eat many different things and hence are much better than any farm fish. We enjoyed the trout fish pit stop nonetheless.

Once we left the fish farm, our jeep descended into the valley's river bed. It was all white sand and we zoomed through a raised jeep sand track with white sand all around us. For a moment we thought we were passing through a white sand desert. We approached the wide and fast rhythmic river Shayok, a subsidiary to the great Indus river which flows from Siachen India. It was not ravaging scary, but it was just fast scary. There was one wooden hanging bridge on it. Our jeep waited its turn, and once we were on it, the planks on the bridge twitched, and the bridge swayed. By then, we had learned to rely on these bridges and not to think too much about what-if's but this bridge would just not end. The driver sped through the bridge as if we all would turn into stone if he stopped for any reason.

As the bridge ended, we merged into Ladakh Skardu road. It was a real road now. It was a great relief. Now, Saad had to let go his window hanging post as there would be cross traffic that could hit him. We had left Hushe River or rather Hushe River had merged into Shyok River. Shyok River would remain on our right side until it merged into Indus River. Soon we were in the outskirts of Khaplu town. We then took a left turn into Khaplu town and went up the narrow streets and small bazaars leading to the Khaplu Fort. Khaplu Fort was a landmark historic building and we did not want to miss it.

Khaplu and Khaplu Fort

We were coming from the remote wilderness and Khaplu felt crowded though it was a town of 82,000 people only. Town of 82,000 inhabitant is considered tiny in respect to Pakistan's population. Khaplu had a fair share of dust and some trash mainly due to it being a populous town, but overall you could see waterfalls, streams, wheat fields, fruit gardens, and tall scenic trees in abundance. These streams ran along roads and through the houses. The creeks and waterfalls were an extension of the community and were sparingly utilized by its inhabitants. We could see women washing their clothes alongside waterfalls. Stone and wood were the main ingredients for the construction, but now we could also see some concrete and iron in the structures.

Khaplu Fort, highlight of Khaplu town, was originally constructed in 1840 by Raja Daulat Ali Khan and it was in use until the late 1970's by the last Raja Fateh Ali Khan. It was in a dilapidated state until the Aga Khan Trust for Culture took an undertaking in 2005 to restore its architectural heritage. It now serves as a museum to tourists and it had its top floor transformed into a stylish hotel operated by Serena Hotels. A room can be rented for Rs. 15,000 to 25,000 (150-250 USD) for a night in a palace which was a royal residence not so long ago. The building was on a raised stone foundation and was a mix of timber, mud brick, and coffee colored clay.

Once our jeep parked outside the fort, we walked toward the entrance. There was big a heavily-carved massive wooden front gate which was hard to move. We used the side gate to enter. We were met with men in white pristine *shalwar qamees* wearing black vests and white woolen caps with a large feather sticking out from the cap. They were cleaner and better dressed than us, and they were polite too. The ticket was Rs. 200 (2 USD) for each. There was a nice open hallway with an entrance to the well-furnished hotel lobby to our left and an entrance to the fort in front.

Once our tickets were checked, we were let into the front courtyard of the fort. The fort's front woodwork was the dominating part of the structure. The woodwork would start from the stairs and would go all the way to the fourth floor with a decent sized balcony on the middle floor. The fort did not appear lavish or extravagant, but it did have a personality worthy of its reputation.

All of us were like kids in a park. We were in the civilized world and a palace, and we were like a bunch of crazies running around. One of the museum staff had gone to school with Imran, our guide and cook, and they were good friends. He became our de facto host and showed us around and spilled out the secrets of the Raja dynasty who used to live in the palace and ruled Baltistan. He told us how cruel they were and so on and so on.

We visited the prison for the people who would not agree with the Raja. We visited fort's kitchen, their bedroom, courtyard, hallways, and servant rooms. It was overall very cozy, and the doors were relatively way too short in height. These doors were kept low so that the people who entered would automatically bow to the Rajas. Well, we were entering and bowing, but there was no Raja. Time had changed; it was the time for the people who paid two hundred rupees to run around the palace asking silly questions.

The palace was on a hilltop, so the views were fantastic. There was a side structure that served as a restaurant, but that was closed that day. We tried our best to woo our host to show us the top floor rooms just for the heck of it, but he didn't budge. A Pakistan government minister was supposed to visit that day with some foreign delegation, so there were restrictions that day. In fact, that minister and his entourage arrived while we were touring the palace. A guard of honor presentation was given to the minister by ten well-dressed policemen with red ribbons on their pants and rifles in their hands. We mischievously stood behind the minister and tried to confuse the policemen, a staff member rushed towards us and hustled us away.

Back to Skardu

I believe by 4 p.m., we were back on Khaplu Skardu Road. The road became much nicer, and there were long stretches without a single pothole. At that time, we discovered that the jeep couldn't do more that 25 miles per hour regardless of the quality of road, so we estimated that we would be in Skardu when we could be in Skardu. The Shyok River was continuously flowing on our right side. It was mainly a brown area: brown mountains, brown river, and coffee color sand. There were some green patches of fields and farms whenever there was a small settlement, on either side of the river.

We were stopped at a check post where the Shyok River was merging into the Indus River. The River Indus was coming from the left side and was very small relatively speaking. I thought that the Indus River should be merging into the Shyok River, not the other way around. At the check post, Munna handed the list of his team to the police and police repeatedly asked if there was any foreigner on the team. A policeman in charge looked worried. Munna talked to him on the side and later told us that there were reports that a guy was on the run and was suspected of spying. The suspected guy was from Nepal and all the check posts in the region were on alert.

The BC Hotel

Road then split: one branch went to Kargil alongside incoming the Indus River and one to Skardu. We stuck to the road to Skardu, and now the Indus River was on our right side instead of the Shyok River which was now the Indus River. We made it to Skardu by 7 p.m. or so, and the hotel we were to stay was Baltistan Continental Hotel initialed as BC Hotel. Initials of the hotel amused us. BC was short for a common abusive name calling in Pakistan. We all thought what a BC hotel it was. We all laughed at the name, and we probably deserved that BC hotel. That BC hotel was still a blessing. It had a bed with a mattress, there were electric lights, and there was a bathroom with running water. There was a television too, and for a moment we thought who needed a television.

Once settled, we then had a quick meeting with Ishaq, our tour operator, in the BC Hotel. He came by to check on us and tried to get our feedback. We had some minor things to settle such as who to pay the CKNP fee and Bakra money etc. It was quite easily settled. Ishaq was very accommodating and shared the news that Hashim who was rescued from the Gondogoro La had been airlifted to CMH (Combined Military Hospital) in Rawalpindi, a large metropolis next to Islamabad, and was making a significant recovery. We felt relieved. As per Ishaq, he helped Hashim's logistic matters despite the fact that he was with the different team.

I gave my two cents to Ishaq as well. I criticized him regarding lack of a satellite phone and the lack of screening and orientation for the first timers. I hope I got my message across.

Dewan-e-Khas Dinner

We, as a team, planned a surprise thank you dinner for Munna, our guide, and his ever hard working team. Asim had once been to a restaurant called *Dewan-e-Khas* (meaning special hall in the Urdu language) in Skardu long time ago that he wouldn't stop bragging about during the entire trip. We knew we had to go there at least once or else face Asim's endless rant, "You gotta try its soup man."

We walked through the dark but wide streets of Skardu towards Dewan-e-Khas. A nearby large mosque was busy, and event that late a sermon could be heard through loudspeakers. I believed it was one the religious gatherings for the mourning of Imam Hasan and Imam Hussein. The shops were closed, and we could see ATM's and bank and some trendy shops. Skardu did have some modern spoils.

Once settled at the Dewan-e-Khas restaurant, we asked our guests, the porters, to order what they would like. They were not used to ordering food and that overwhelmed them. Nauman S. and I took charge and ordered what we think would feed twenty people with good decent food variety. Munna and his team enjoyed the dinner and so did we, especially the Balti dishes. After the dinner, we had tea at a roadside tea stall. We sat on the side road, almost literally. We chatted and then said our farewells to Munna and his team.

We walked back to our BC hotel and crashed. It was our last night in the mountains or at least that's what we hoped so.

Figure 37: Top left: Khaplu Fort; Top right: The team styling in front of Khaplu Fort entrance; Bottom right: Police squad, at Khaplu Fort, presenting guard of honors to the guests (photos by Salman Zakir)

17

GETTING OUT OF SKARDU

Given the experience of twenty-four to thirty hours of a bumpy bus ride with the annoying *shehri babu* group, I was desperate to catch the next day flight. Everyone told us that it was peak season and flights were overbooked, and it would be such a waste of time because there were only one or possibly two small aircraft flights per day. Every one of us had tried to reserve a seat and some of us even tried their connections with airlines, but no luck.

Some wise man said that 85% of success is in showing up. And that's what we did that morning. We showed up at the Skardu Airport. Shami, Kashif, Asim, and I checked out from BC Hotel early morning and were at the airport by 7 a.m. The flight time was 8:30 a.m. Airport security wouldn't let us into the terminal building without a flight ticket. I saw a small building close by. I walked up there and went inside. In a room next to the entrance hall, I saw two PIA (Pakistan International Airlines) guys hunched over a computer terminal busy punching the keys. I politely asked them if they could see if there was any chance that the four of us could get some seats. I was counting on no-shows or last minute cancellations. Shami had a separate reservation while Kashif,

Asim, and I were on one reservation. The PIA guys checked the system and said that they could give us three seats in first class. Before he could finish his sentence, I said we would take it. The price difference was a little expensive, but I was dying to go home. I told Kashif and Asim that I would take on the difference between economy class and first class for them as a courtesy. It was an additional 80 USD approximately, so it was not that big of a deal for me given the circumstances, but I knew it could create a decent dent in their budget.

Pay it Forward

Even though three of us secured our seats, Shami was left out because his reservation was separate and was for another date. I encouraged him to try his luck too, to have a seat changed to today's flight. I sent him to the same building and the same room that I went in earlier. He asked the same gentlemen for a seat. They did find a seat for him, but Shami was short of cash for the price difference and could not make the purchase. He came back empty handed. All of us checked our pockets, and we could not come up with the required cash. Shami had to let go of the seat and the flight. It was unfortunate that after we had come that far, Shami would be turned back.

I asked Shami to go in the building one more time and ask those same PIA guys if they could do something with the cash which Shami had in his hands. Shame went in. We waited nervously outside the building and had our fingers crossed. After ten minutes smiling Shami emerged and told us excitedly that he would be traveling with us. PIA guys had given him a favor, and when Shami asked their address to send them the balance money, they said that just pay it forward. That was incredible!

We rushed through check-in and then security to make sure the airplane didn't leave without us. We all were glad that we were not going back to that BC Hotel.

Scenic Flight to Islamabad

The flight from Skardu to Islamabad was the most scenic flight I have ever taken. Our Airbus A320 jet, carrying 150 passengers, took off sharp from Skardu Airport. It then glided through Karakoram range and then the Himalayas at approximately thirty thousand feet altitude. Seeing all the peaks from the sky above was like walking on water while seeing the depths below. The best was when the jet flew over Nanga Parbat. It was a big mountain and the aircraft flew at least five minutes over it. I felt I could scoop the snow from the peak. This view was literally up close bird's eye view of the majestic Nanga Parbat. Just for that five minutes view flight was totally worth it.

In just forty-five minutes, before we could digest the sandwich and the tea, we landed at Islamabad Airport. It was still the morning, but we could feel the hot and humid weather already. My cousin, Shahzad, was at the airport to pick us up. We were back to the hustle bustle of the metropolis in a mere forty-five minutes. It would take much more time to digest the change then we had imagined. The roads, the freeways, electricity, internet, cell phone, air conditioning, refrigerators, restaurants, endless markets, rickshaws, taxis, cycles, Toyota Corollas, Honda CD 70 motorbikes, the metro, the high rises, the underpasses, and then the bridges and the ramps all made me dizzy. I was in a wonderland of a different sort.

After a traditional celebratory breakfast of *halwa puri* (flour bread deep fried, *puri*, served with hot sweet, *halwa*) and *chanay* (chickpeas curry), Shami took off to catch a bus for his hometown. Kashif also left for his home in Multan right after the breakfast feast. Asim was already home, as he was based out of Islamabad.

It was Sunday, July 31st, when we landed at Islamabad. I had an entire one week before my scheduled flight back to California. Salman and Nauman S. were also able to make it back to Islamabad the next day when they took a chance and showed up at the Skardu Airport. They took the lead from us, but they were a day behind. They later told us that spending a day in Skardu without the gang was very tough and boring. Nauman S. and Salman had took off for Lahore the same day they arrived in Islamabad. The other Nouman joined his other friends in Gilgit but took a flight back from Gilgit to Islamabad and was in Lahore within days. He was home sick and had canceled his future adventures with other friends for now.

For two days, I hibernated and I didn't step out of the room in my sister's house in Islamabad where I was staying. After waking up in a day or so, I tried to reschedule my seat to San Francisco, but it would cost me at least $2,000. I dropped the idea of rescheduling like a hot potato. I decided to hit the road for next few days. I bought a bus ticket for Lahore and spent two days there seeing friends and family. The two Nouman's and Salman from the trip who were the true Lahorites took me out for a nice fancy dinner. I also caught up with old Fast (my computer university) class fellows. I then covered Sargodha, Mirpur, and Abbottabad in two days or so and tried to see whomever I thought would be happy to see me or whoever I thought I would be happy to see.

18

GETTING BACK TO CALIFORNIA

Well, you might think how difficult would it be to get to California from Islamabad, Pakistan. Go to the airport on time, board your scheduled flight, change a flight or two and that would be it. It's usually long hours and tiresome but not impossible, right? However, for me, it had always become mission impossible for one reason or the other. Read on, and you will know why.

Islamabad to Bangkok

My first flight was a Thai Airways red eye flight to Bangkok from Islamabad. It had rained that day and I was glad that I enjoyed the summer monsoon rain just in time. I was able to catch up with a bunch of friends in Islamabad. My sister turned out to be an excellent host, and I felt like I was home but time had come to leave.

I was at the airport about two hours and thirty minutes early. Security was smooth, but check-in was complicated. Although my ticket had two baggage allowances, Thai Airways showed only one. Thai Airways station manager was called. After twenty minutes of scratching his head, he and his team were able to check me in, eventually.

The Hajj (Muslims' annual pilgrimage) season was on. Airport departure lounge was full of aspiring Hajjis all dressed in a white two pieces unstitched dress. It was so cute to watch them. I also noticed a fair skin, skinny girl in the lounge. She looked different than the rest of the crowd and was by herself. She resembled someone I know in San Francisco Bay Area but I knew that could not be her.

I had almost two hours to spend. I made a couple of phone calls to friends and family and next thing I knew I was on a Thai Airways airplane to Bangkok. It was a half-full flight. As I settled into my seat, I noticed that the same girl that I had seen in the lounge walked towards me and pointed to the seat next to me and claimed that seat was hers. She tried to show me her boarding pass too but who was I to object. "Aur Khuda ki kon kon se nametoon ko jhutlao gay (how many more blessings from God you would deny)".

It did not take much time to start a conversation with her. Her name was Sumbal. She was a 23 years old young electrical engineer working at PTV (Pakistan Television Network) possibly as an intern for one year. She was now heading to Myanmar, previously known as Burma, to meet her husband. She had a connecting flight from Bangkok. Her husband was from the US and was working at Apple in the San Francisco Bay Area, my hometown. Her husband was on a work trip to Burma. They were having a couple's reunion in Burma, how romantic! She could not travel to the US because of her immigration status. She was awaiting her immigration to the US. Once she was okayed by the US Department of Homeland Security, she would move to the Bay Area, but for now, Burma was her only hope to see her husband. I told her if she ever comes to the San Francisco area then we would meet again as that's my hometown and I was very popular there.

Then she asked about me, my work and my trip, etc. She got excited when she learned I went to the K2 Basecamp. She told me she had been a climber too and had wanted to do some serious climbing, especially as the first Pakistani teenager. But she thought she was too late as she was 23 now. I asked what climbs she had done, and she said that she had climbed Margalla Hills once. Margalla Hills are the two thousand to three thousand feet high hills surrounding Islamabad. I thought she was joking, but she was damn serious. I let that slide.

Then came the "Samaj ki Dewar (Society wall)." steward in our conversation and asked Sumbal to change her seat as she sat on someone else's seat. Then she moved to a seat ahead of me, and that was it. She came, she sat and then she disappeared. As if she had never existed. That's the thing about traveling. You meet people to never see them again the moment they move out of the seat next to you.

As the airplane took off, I instantly started missing my family and friends in Pakistan. It is said that you cry two times in Pakistan, first when you go there and second when you leave. I knew then that it was so true. I cried in my heart quietly. For some unknown reasons I took coffee at midnight in mid-air and I was up staring at the jet's roof until the plane landed in Bangkok. For some additional unknown reasons, I was listening to "Aashiqui" the movie music. Damn altitude!

Bangkok

We landed, at Bangkok, 5 a.m. or so. To my surprise, I ran into Sumbal and to my further surprise, she said she had been looking for me. Before I could understand a thing, she told me she had no idea where to go next and desperately needed help as there was not much time left for next flight. This was her first international travel, and she needed me for guidance in transiting to her next flight. I checked her boarding pass as if I was the king of international transits. I walked her to her transit point. I guessed some passenger had misguided her that she needed a visa to transit and that had gotten her confused and hence she searched for me. She thanked me and before her tears would roll off her eyes I said bye and told her that we would meet soon in San Francisco Bay Area, subject to her immigration approval.

I had a total of five hours in Bangkok, and I decided to get out of the airport and catch some fresh air. I went through immigration, which was pleasant and very professional. I walked to the train service following the signs. It was 7 a.m. I bought tokens from a kiosk for a round trip. An empty train arrived. There was security personnel at each gate of the train. They checked the train before anybody could board. I was able to grab a seat next to two well-dressed ladies. Don't get me wrong. Women were in the majority and that was the only seat I could find. By the next station, the train cars were jam-packed. Security personnel helped people fit into the cars. It was a little uncomfortable, but it seemed to be the norm. Ladies were comfortable standing or sitting close to men. And everybody was well behaved and had their heads bowed to their cell phones. I off boarded the train at the last station of the airport train line, Paya Thai. I then started walking towards what seemed to be the downtown. It was hard to ask for directions due to the language difference and because I did not have any specific directions to ask for. I then bought Thai guava and pineapple from a local stall for 20 baht for each fruit.

There were plenty of Thai rickshaws and scooter motorcycles on the road. The scooter and motorcycles also acted as rent a ride. People, especially women, would walk up to the motorbike rider and asked if they were available for a ride. And off they would go. It was like rent-a-motorbike ride. I thought it was smart because bikes could maneuver through traffic more quickly. I also asked for a ride from one of the bikers and asked if he could take me to Bangkok downtown. After some serious consideration, he agreed to take me for 50 Baht.

After a mile or two, he stopped in front of a hotel named Bangkok Hotel. I told him that this was not what I meant. He shook his head and drove for a mile more and stopped in front of Bangkok Bank branch. I explained to him this was not what I meant and how about he drop me where he picked me up. He shook his head and was annoyed and gave me a look that even if I offer him million baht, he will not take me anywhere. I took the hint and got off his bike. Paid him 50 Baht as agreed. I was all by myself on random streets of Bangkok. Luckily, I noticed train tracks a few blocks away. It was late already, and I needed to start moving towards the airport. As usual, I did not want to miss my flight in a country out of route to the U.S.

I noticed mostly women on their way to work or school. They were in skirts, shorts, pants, fashionable makeup, and few in a scarf. Some were in military uniform, navy, infantry, and some were in school uniform, white shirt, and black knee-length skirts. Some were very pretty and some were just pretty. Most were fair-skinned and were busy going about their business. Saw two women in running shorts and tank tops, most likely there was a park nearby. I noticed men too, but there were not many men and they didn't seem very manly. The men were either boyish or old.

There were apartment buildings all around. They weren't too many but enough to provide a dense city look. A few markets with tin sheds could be seen at random blocks. I walked into a small side street. I saw coffee stalls, breakfast stalls, fried egg and rice in a packet, rice, and mangoes, mangoes juice, locally grown vegetables, figs (maybe), peanuts, noodle soup. Man, it was hard to see a pattern! The side street was quiet, mainly because it was early for the markets. People who had jobs to show up at and the young crowd who had school to go to, were hustling and bustling.

Off to Xian, China

I caught the train from the Paya Thai station just in time. Again, security personnel went inside each train car and checked and cleared cars before anybody could board. I guess the Thai King and Thai police take security very seriously. I got back to the airport around 10 a.m. The boarding started little late, but now it was painfully slow. The line was not moving at all. The counter lady was busy, but nothing moved. I lost my patience and was about to throw a tantrum but I realized my mistake. I was in line for a group check-in. The counter lady was processing twenty passports. It looked like group travel was so popular that there was a separate check-in counter for the groups. I could see the same pattern for all other airlines check-in counters. I changed the line to the non-group boarding, and I was done in twenty-five minutes. Again, the question of two pieces of baggage came up. I was taken to a different counter, and my luggage was confirmed and I was finally given my boarding pass. I needed to collect my luggage at my next stop: Xi'an, China. I then spent the next twenty-five minutes in immigration lines. I was in the gate area for boarding, eventually. I shopped for souvenirs. I wanted to spend all 450 Baht that I got for my 20 US bucks. I had spent some 90 Baht on train ride and 40 Baht on fruits already.

The majority of the crowd at the departure lounge were Asian. Unlike, at arrival in Bangkok Airport where it felt like the entire Middle East with their families had flown to Bangkok for family partying. Now at departure, I felt all of the Thailand and China were traveling. I was the only foreigner in flight. It was a five hour flight from Bangkok to Xian, China. Drinks and lunch were served too. I mostly slept, ate lunch, and had orange juice after orange juice.

Xi'an

The flight landed around 5 p.m. in Xi'an, China. I was the only different looking foreigner in the immigration lines, and it was making me nervous. I could sense that they do not receive many transit visitors. Anyways, the immigration officer was confused too. She wanted to know my hotel info my purpose of visit etc. I showed her my next flight ticket. Then, she called her supervisor. Both scratched their heads then the supervisor took my passport. They asked me to step back and wait. Immigration counter started moving other passengers, and I waited on the side. I saw five immigration officers in the back huddled together with my passport and they were all scratching their heads. After ten minutes, one of the officers disappeared with my passport and the group dibursed. I presumed someone went inside to make some calls to talk to Obama to verify that I was a US citizen and why.

After ten more minutes, a young officer walked towards me and asked why I was there. I said I was transiting through as per my itinerary. He went through my itinerary line by line. He asked what I did in Beijing. I told him that I just spent three hours at the Beijing Airport. He then asked me where my visa to China was. I said I was in the airport and transited through transit counters and didn't go outside and hence no immigration and visa needed. Then he asked about Pakistan, Bangkok and questioned why Xi'an. I did my best to summarize my link to Pakistan and US and my purpose of visit to Pakistan. I told him I have family in Pakistan and the US. I was just trying to go to the U.S., my home on my paid ticket. He disappeared and signaled me to wait. Another fifteen minutes passed, and one more flight's passengers went through immigration. Immigration officer came back and asked me to follow him. I somehow knew I would be in there for long haul. Somehow someone was not convinced of my purpose of showing up at Xi'an Airport.

Flying out of Pakistan always raise all sorts of red flags. I always try to be a good sport as I understand what was at stake but this time it looked more than simple questioning.

The Interrogation

Immigration officer walked me through the offices in the back and led me to a small room which had one desk and one chair in it. It was definitely a holding room or the interrogation room. There was one paper and a pen on the table. I decided no matter what would happen, I would not sign any paper, especially in Chinese. I didn't want to confess to anything that I didn't or couldn't do.

He started his questioning again. "You have any other form of identification?" he asked in broken English. I showed him my California driving license and my Pakistani national ID card. Then I explained him my dual citizenship to him. He asked me my address in the US, and I pointed to my driving license. He asked about my address in Pakistan, and I pointed to my Pakistan national ID card.

Now, one more immigration officer joined. His name was Ying Ying as per his name badge. I thought it should be Ying Yang, but I kept my thoughts to myself. Ying Ying stayed silent and just observed. His silence was creepy enough. He was there to tackle me if I were to make a run, I guessed. The first immigration officer asked me to remove my shoes and inspected my shoes and socks. Then he asked for my wallet. He took everything out of it while Ying Ying squinted his squinted eyes.

"What is it?" he asked holding the cash from my wallet. I said, " It's cash, some Pakistani rupees, some Thai Baht and some US dollars." He then literally asked me for every item. My responses were "it's a picture of my kid,"; "This is my Costco grocery store card,"; "Costco is where you buy our groceries in the US, etc."; "This is my medical insurance card," and "These are my credit cards Visa and Master."

Then he asked me to stand on the feet marks and put my hands on the hand marks on the wall. I knew they would search me inch by inch. I was ready to strip as I presumed that would come next. I would had stripped down butt naked even though if they had asked me to take off my shirt. I didn't want to show any nervousness. My attitude was like: bring it, buddy, let's see what you got, I know what I got. I was patted down but not stripped down, unfortunately but fortunately.

He then took my cell phone and asked me to unlock it. He then welcomed himself to looking at my pictures. Who was this? Who was that? What was that place? were his repeating questions. "This was K2.", "These are my nephews.", "This is Baltoro Glacier.", "These are trekkers." etc. were my answers. He stopped at one picture of mine with GoPro camera mounted on my head. He exclaimed "Ah, GoPro!" He couldn't find any Chinese espionage pictures or any of my selfies that I usually take when I murder somebody. I was glad I didn't take any pictures of any kind in China at all.

He then asked me to open my backpack. He asked me to go through each item. I showed him my packable rain jacket which asked me to open it. I opened it. I went item-by-item, and this was how it went: that's my pajama, my t-shirt, that's tiger balm, that's Tylenol, and that's GoPro, and that's GoPro mounts. He again said, "Ah, GoPro! I like GoPro." It looked like we were bonding on GoPro and his love of GoPro could buy me get out of jail card. Then he took aside my charging power bank, my earphones, and my phone charging cables. He then held the power bank in his hands and gazed down at it. It looked like the power bank connected with him telepathically and revealed its contents to him. It was all lithium, my charger told him telepathically, I assumed. He let it go finally.

Then there were my memory cards, and I cringed, what if he wanted to see what was in there. There were 64 gigabytes of pictures and videos, and it could take hours to go through. He exclaimed, "Ah GoPro memory cards!" I said "Yes, yes GoPro" and he moved on to other items. I couldn't believe my luck.

When there were no more items to see then he decided to step out of the interrogation room to go talk to his boss. "I will be back," he said Arnold-style and disappeared into the hallway. It was now just "Ying Ying" and me and the room. It was "Ying Ying"'s turn now and he started his questions.

"Which company?" he asked. They had asked me many times, so I took out paper and wrote down "Qiagen" in big eligible letters, and he quickly Googled it and confirmed. "What do you do? Write software?" I said "Kind of."

"Is Qiagen a software company?" he asked,

"No."

"What Qiagen do?" he asked,

"It's a Biotech company, and I am part of one group that writes software," I replied.

"Are you manager?", he continued.

"No," I said.

"Did you go to college in the US?"

"No."

"Where did you go college?"

"Pakistan."

"So you went college in Pakistan, then the job in the US?"

"No."

"So where did you go to the US from?"

"Saudi Arabia," I said.

"Where is Saudi Arabia?"

"In Middle East"

"Where is the Middle East?"

I stared him back with blank look, and before I could search the answer in my brain, he resumed

"In Europe?".

"No," I replied.

"In Asia?", he continued.

"Yes, sort of. It is close to North Africa."

I took my pen out and wrote "Saudi Arabia" on paper in big letters and let him Google it.

"Ah, Saudi Arabia!" he finally figured it out. I was glad he had a cell phone with a data plan.

"So what you did in Saudi Arabia."

"I wrote Software for a rent-a-car company."

"What is rent a car?" He asked.

"You know Avis or Hertz?" I paused and asked.

He was blank.

I continued, "Ok let's say you need a car for a day or two and a company has the cars, you pay that company to borrow the car. That company which lets you borrow is called rent-a-car".

He nodded his head, but he was still processing. I wrote

down my rent-a-car company name and wrote: "rent a car" for him. He Googled "rent a car" term and showed me link "carrental.com" and asked if I worked there. I said no and pointed him to the paper where I have written my company name. He Googled it, but couldn't find it and this time he has given up on my ex-employer.

"Ok, so you went to the US from Saudi?

"Yes."

"How did you get the US passport?"

"Company I worked for did all the processing for me."

He paused and tried to digest.

"Ah, so you a software engineer?"

"Yes, sort of." There are a lot of Chinese software engineer in the Silicon Valley, so he was probably familiar with this profession more, I didn't want to explain to him what databases were and what I do with them.

"Are there many Pakistani engineers in the US?"

"There are enough but not as much as Chinese and Indians."

"I know there are a lot of Indian engineers," he remarked.

"Well, there are more Chinese than Indians," I continued on Chinese Indian angle.

"Okay, now you live in apartment?", he changed the subject.

"No, I live in a house," I replied.

"Which car?", he asked.

"GMC," I said.

"Ah, GMC. The big car", he remarked.

"Where is your family," he asked

"In US," I replied

"You can sit down now," he said.

"I am fine thanks," I replied.

He then insisted. I sat down on the only chair in the room. It was a revolving chair and I slowly turned away from him. With my back to him, I was hoping to signal him to give me a break. He could speak poor basic English, so it was not a pleasant conversation at all, there were a lot of "I am sorry" and "excuse me" moments from my side.

The Release

"Sir, you can go. Collect your stuff." The guy who had disappeared appeared again and told me in Chinese English. I didn't know what it meant. I could go back to Thailand or Islamabad, or I was okay to proceed with my transit? I didn't dare to ask. He led me to the same counter where this chain of questioning started. I told the counter lady I was back and she smiled. My handler handed my passport to the counter and disappeared. Lady started processing and then stopped and yelled something in Chinese in the direction where my handler had disappeared. He shouted back with some instructions, she nodded and took out a stamp from a locked box and stamped my passport.

Whatever was done was done. Then the side gate of the counter opened, and she handed me my passport and pointed me towards small side gate. The gate, where I had seen dozens of passengers pass through while I stood on the side and watched, was finally open for me to pass through. On the counter, the feedback rating lights started flashing with levels of smiley faces and sad faces. I wanted to press the saddest face, but I realized it was only me in the big hall and all other were immigration staff, eyes fixated on me as there were no other passengers around.

I had twelve more hours to spend in Xi'an, so I ignored the feedback faces and walked through the small side gates and walked past the immigration staff, supervisor, handler, and the interrogator.

"This way, sir." He said, and I smiled and said thank you very much from the bottom of my heart. One of the perks of being interviewed or interrogated is that you do not have to wait for the baggage. Baggage is collected for you by airline staff and kept on the side for you. Airlines need to clear the luggage belts as soon as they could. I collected my baggage and walked towards customs.

Xi'an Customs

As if immigration was not enough, the custom lady had lots of questions too. She had me open my bag which was plastic wrapped. They gave me cutter to cut the plastic. She asked, "Why do you have a drum in your bag?" I said " I don't know, my wife asked for it." I was asked to take everything out of the bag. My stuff was all over the counter and some fell on the floor. Then her question came "Why Islamabad San Francisco." I was confused. She asked another lady to help explain her question. It turned out she wanted to know why I was traveling through Xi'an. Why not take a direct flight from Islamabad to San Francisco? I told her that there were no direct flights from Islamabad to San Francisco because of the distance. She selected certain items and re-scanned through the x-ray machine. After a few more re-scans, she signaled that she was done. I repacked all my stuff on the floor and walked out like a beaten tired man.

15 hours at Xi'an International Terminal

As I walked out, a taxi driver tagged along as if we have known each other for years. He was offering a room and a taxi ride to the hotel for 280 Chinese Yen, approximately 50 USD. I said no and kept saying no and he kept pestering. After immigration and customs experience I didn't feel like spending time in this city and didn't know if I would be welcomed in the town. Taxi driver eventually got tired and cursed in Chinese and left. It was interesting that I didn't know the Chinese language, but I could tell when the taxi driver cursed and called me names.

Xi'an, most populous city of Northwest China, is historical city and was worth visiting. Especially the museum of Qin Shi Huang intrigued me. The museum had thousands of sculptures of Terracotta Army from 210-209 BC. Sculptures of army was a form of funerary art in which army was supposed to protect the emperor in after life. Also my Chinese friend had told me that there were beautiful mountains around Xian. If my transit was during day time then I would had definitely ventured out. Thank you United Airlines!

I roamed around through the International terminal and saw a Pizza Hut. I felt immediate connection with Pizza Hut and had dinner there. At least the money will somehow go back to the United States. At the departure terminal, I claimed three bench chairs as my home for the night. I stretched my legs on bench chairs and counted my hours to my next flight. There were cabinets like rooms in terminal available to rent for sleep on hourly basis. There was a small bed in the small enclosure. It was too suffocating for me, and I said no thank you and closed my eyes.

I Want To Go Home and Nobody is Stopping Me

Time passed, as it always does. Nothing unusual or inappropriate happened and the next morning I was in the United Airlines flight to San Francisco with the regular, predicted hustle. All the passengers were Chinese except for one white guy sitting a few rows ahead of me and me. The white guy had long blonde hair and had tattoos. A Chinese ground staff was hovering the white man asking him to off-board the airplane. I thought white man was being judged for his looks.

"Sir, you have to off-board the plane." the Chinese staff asked.

"Why?" said the white guy keeping his calm.

"Sir, you look sick. It's a long flight, and we cannot let you fly", Chinese man insisted.

"Are you a physician, a doctor?", asked the white guy.

"No," replied the staff.

"Then, I am not sick," said the white guy.

"Sir, you are sick you need to off-board," staff insisted.

"Bring in the physician and let him decide," the white guy insisted.

"Physician is on his way. You need to off-board", staff repeated.

"No I am not sick, and you are not a doctor." white guy replied.

There was a brief pause and then the white guy said "I want to go home and nobody is stopping me" raising his voice with each word he uttered. He reminded me off Mel Gibson of the movie Braveheart in which Mel finally said "Freeedom!" at the climax scene before getting his head chopped off in defiance.

The Chinese guy pestered the white guy for some time but the white man stood his ground, or I should say he remained glued to his seat. I quietly rooted for the white guy. I kind of felt his frustration and also wanted to get to home no matter what. The flight was delayed because of that hustle, but it took off eventually. The white guy was not off-boarded. Small victories in life matter.

The Boeing jet was brand new and had in-flight entertainment, and this was very unlike an American Airlines. The flight attendants were all American. They all came to me and asked if I was the same guy that was escorted off by the Chinese authorities from yesterday's flight. They mistook me for someone else, but I could guess that Xi'an was not only unfriendly to me but for many others as well. San Francisco was still thirteen hours away!

19

GETTING BACK TO ROUTINE IN SILICON VALLEY

"Sir, welcome to the United States. Where are you coming from?", asked the immigration officer at San Francisco Airport.

"Pakistan," I replied.
"What was your purpose of visit?", he asked.

"Some vacation, some family," I said and anxiously waited for his next question. His next question would indicate if I would be spending hours at the airport in immigration controls or I would be breezing out. Usually, I am asked to tell them which cities I had been to in Pakistan? How long I stayed in each city? Did I go to Afghanistan, Iran, or the tribal areas of Pakistan? Did I own a property in the U.S.? Did I have a business card? Did I know Osama? etc. My passport would then be taken to get checked against myriad of the security agencies databases.

I was in Pakistan's remote Karakoram range for a fifteen days backpacking with no city nearby. China, India and

Afghanistan were in 300 miles range of the region I had just been to. So lots of question could be raised. Immigration had gotten little better since I had been blessed with U.S. citizenship two years ago. But still, how was I to explain that I travelled thousands of miles from the U.S. to Pakistan, and then trekked 85 miles just to see the K2. I held my breath and waited for immigration officer's next question.

"How are they (family) doing over there?", he asked.

"They are fine. They were happy to see me first but then I overstayed my welcome. I think I stretched my stay", I replied with a smile. Smart ass geek in me sprung to life .

"Ha! Ha! I am glad you made it back. Welcome home!" He chuckled.

"Thanks, it's good to be back," I said. He knew I meant it.

Going through the U.S. Immigration was as breeze as the landing of the United Airline's Boeing 787 Dreamliner at the San Francisco Airport. The weather was pleasant with zero humidity. My friend Azmi was at the airport to pick me up. I had to be at work in the next two hours, and I was late already. At home, my boys and my only wife welcomed me with cards and flowers. I was overwhelmed. After four weeks of absence from their life, I was with them only for an hour and took off for work. I felt guilty, but I knew I would eventually make the time up.

I was in a zombie-like a state at work all day long. I didn't bother to have coffee that day. I knew it would be torture on coffee. I didn't recall whom I talked that day, what I said, and what I did. Eventually, that day passed too.

It took me some time to get back into the daily grind in the Silicon Valley. But to be honest, to this day I still hope to step on a glacier each day I step out of my house. I found it harder to sleep on the bed. Floors give me a better sleep now.

I haven't gone out for a single hike since my return. No trail is rough enough for me now. I find it hard to have a regular discussion. I have lost weight, and my body have toned. My mind quickly drifts back to those days at a higher altitude. I have to make a conscious effort to focus on things close to me. I think those Karakoram mountains have possessed me. I eat, drink, sleep here in the U.S., but my heart and mind are still back in those wild, untamed mountains.

-The End

APPENDIX A

STAGES, ELEVATION AND MILEAGE

This appendix will give you an idea what to anticipate when you plan for Concordia-K2-Gondogoro La trek. Here you have the stages and destinations with a brief description and the scoop on how to get there and what to expect. In addition, it could be your pseudo itinerary, if you desire. Destinations are listed in the order that we travelled and trekked.

Check http://www.cknp.org for latest trekking fees and permit options.

Islamabad:
>   The capitol city of Pakistan. Modern city with modern amenities. A green city surrounded by Margalla hills. Entry point for international expeditions. A lot to see in Islamabad itself. All international embassies are in Islamabad. Good place to shave off jet lag and arrange for last minute items while enjoying great food.

Skardu:
>   8,000 ft. Populous Karakoram town with modern amenities. Approximately 400 miles from Islamabad via Naran. 18-24 hours windy bus ride. 45 minutes flight from Islamabad, operated by PIA (Pakistan International Airlines). Flights in season only and weather dependent.

Askole:
>   9,850 ft. Trailhead town for Concordia trek. 6-8 hours of bumpy jeep ride on narrow jeep track from Skardu.

Korofong:

10,147 ft. First stage on the trek. Day 1 lunch break. Some shade on the stage. Semi clean stream water is available. 7 miles of a trek along Braldu Nala from Askole. Some steep ascents and descents with drops to Braldu. No shade. Drinkable stream water available at the first 2 miles of the trek. CKNP entry post at first mile after Askole. Need to pay the entry fee in cash and register.

Jhola:

10,300 ft. Second stage. Night stay. Seasonal canteen with some basic amenities available at cost. Italian toilets with close by water filled drums with water from streams nearby. 4.92 miles from Korofong. This is no shade on the trail. No water available on the trek. Refill your water bottles/bladder at Korofong.

Burdumal:

10,500 ft. 3rd Stage. Day 2 Lunch break. No shade on the stage. Semi clean stream water is available. Stonewalled pit toilets in proximity. Seasonal canteen available. 7.5 miles from Jhola. No shade, moderate to a strenuous trail. No water available on the trail. Sharp ascents and descents along Braldu Nala and some sand trail.

Paiyu:

11,055 ft. 4th Stage. Day 2. Two nights stay. Shaded campsite with semi-clean water. Italian toilets along with common water drums. There are seasonal canteens and a mosque, which is worth visiting. 5.34 miles from Burdumal. No shade moderate to strenuous trekking. No water available.

Liligo:

12,188 ft. 5th stage. Day 4. No shade. Water may be available if the streams haven't dried up. No canteens and no toilets; it's just a layover stop. Approximately 6 miles from Paiyu. First 2 miles, trail close to Braldu and then on Baltoro glacier onward. Glacier water at random places can be used for drinking, but discretion is advised. Initially moderate and then strenuous.

Khoburse:

12,441 ft. 6th stage. Day 4. Overnight stay. A decent campsite with seasonal canteen with basic amenities.

Stonewalled pit toilets. Water supply from relatively clean streams. 2.2 miles from Liligo. Strenuous trekking with steep ascents and descents on the glacier with steep drops to glacier lake and exposed Braldu Nala. No shade.

Urdukas:

13,317 ft. 7th stage. Day 5. A decent campsite with seasonal canteen with basic amenities. Italian toilets at some walking distance. Water supply from relatively clean streams. Overlooking Baltoro glacier. 3.5 miles from Khoburse. Strenuous trekking on rocky Baltoro glacier with limited water options. No shade.

Gore-I:

13,773 ft. high. 8th stage. Day 6. No water, no shade and no amenities. Just a rest area. Glacier ice/snow could be melted to consume as the water of needed. 4.7 miles from Urdukas. Strenuous trekking on rocky Baltoro glacier with limited water options. No shade.

Gore-II:

14,098 ft. 9th stage. Day 6. Two raised Italian toilets available. Glacier water source. Overnight stay on Baltoro glacier. 2.43 miles from Gore-I. Strenuous trekking on Baltoro glacier. Ups and downs on the glacier with boulders. Glacier water can be used with caution. Watch out for crevasses.

Concordia:

14,967 ft. 10th stage. Day 7. Scattered campsite on glacier rocks. A seasonal canteen available. Two to three raised Italian toilets. Glacier water source. Overnight stay on Baltoro glacier. 7.52 miles from Gore-II. Strenuous trekking on Baltoro glacier. Ups and downs on the glacier with boulders. Glacier water can be used with caution. Watch out for crevasses.

K-2 Basecamp:

16,350 ft. Day trip from Concordia. 10 hours of trekking via Broad Peak base camp. Approximately 8 miles one way from Concordia. Strenuous glacier treks with limited water options. High altitude can be exhausting. Guide required.

Ali Camp:

16,165 ft. Day 8. No shade. Campsite on a cliff overlooking Vigne glacier. No toilets. Semi clean water supply from streams from mountains. Rest until midnight push to Gondogoro La. 6.36 miles from Concordia. First 2 miles strenuous on exposing glacier. Remainder on straight, gentle uphill ice glacier with running glacier water stream. No other water source on the trail. Watch out for crevasses.

Muneer Camp:

16,497 ft. Day 8. A quick stop area before Gondogoro La ascent. No water, no canteen, no toilets. 1.03 miles from Ali Camp. Moderate to strenuous trekking in the dark and on boulders and some ice. Headlamps and guide required. No water on the trail.

Gondogoro La Top:

18,486 ft. No water, no amenities. Only excellent views! 2.35 miles from Muneer camp. Very strenuous and technical steep climb on snow/ice in the night using fixed ropes. Harness, crampons, gaiters and headlamps required. Steep drops on all sides.

Khuspang:

15,396 ft. Clean water from streams. Canteen with basic amenities and small kitchen. Covered pit toilets with no running water. 2.77 miles from Gondogoro La top. Extremely dangerous descend first two miles. Use fixed rope to rappel down. Sturdy gloves are needed in addition to harness, carabiner, gaiters, and crampons (if ice). Stream water available near Khushpang.

Saicho:

11,600 ft. A decent campsite with large canteen with kitchen. Covered pit toilets with no running water. Moderately clean water from mellow streams. Approximately 10 miles from Khushpang. Moderate to strenuous. First few miles on Gondogoro glacier. Onwards, narrow trail and steep drops at some points. Small streams with rapid currents crossing at two points. Easy trail after Dalsampa.

Hushe:

10,499 ft. Decent size village with a central mosque. Campsite in a hotel yard with proper toilets with running water. There is a restaurant in hotel and multiple grocery shops. All areas at walkable distance. Spotty cellphone reception for the regional cellular company. 6.32 miles from Saicho. Easy hike. Water available at random points from streams and waterfalls.

Skardu:

6-8 hours jeep ride from Hushe via Khaplu. Stop at Kahplu town to visit Khaplu Fort. Night stay in Skardu in hotel.

Islamabad:

Back to Islamabad, either via 45 minutes air plane ride or 30 hours bus ride from Skardu.

Disclaimer: Stages altitude and distance tracking was done using Garmin's vivoactive® HR watch. Garmin's activity tracking accuracy can be seen at http://www.garmin.com/en-US/legal/atdisclaimer.

APPENDIX B

PREPARATION HACKS AND TIPS

Some hacks can come in very handy for your adventures in Concordia and Gondogoro La area of Pakistan. You can also apply these tips and hacks for your other adventures with minor adjustments, of course.

With fifteen days in such a remote wilderness area, you don't want to deal with broken shoes, nonfunctional sleeping bags, ineffective clothing, and prolonged sickness. If you overlook your equipment and quality of equipment, you can easily turn your trip into a nightmare, and there is also a chance that you could put yourself in danger. Settling on a checklist and going through each item, making sure you have the right equipment while keeping everything in the budget, is an art that you can only learn when you embark on such a journey.

Shoes

For your adventure trips, there are certain items that you should not compromise on. On trekking trips especially far off and on a rugged terrain, shoes should be of high quality. Your shoes will get the most of the beating and should be able to survive the roughness of the terrain while keeping your feet clean of any blisters and bruises. Your shoe should grip firm, should be lightweight, thick enough to protect your feet from abrasion, breathable enough to let your feet sweat evaporate, and waterproof enough that you should be able to cross streams and walk on ice or snow. A high-quality shoe is not a wish-list item. If you trek every day for 15-20 miles on a treacherous terrain, you are exposed to the drops, canvases, slippery boulders, pebbles, ice, snow, and streams for longer period of times and this increases your chances of an accident. Feet blisters are very painful and take time to heal. I had blisters during my backpacking trip a few years back, and that pain is still fresh in my memory. I didn't want that to happen again.

Cotton socks are a big no for such adventures. Cotton soaks in the sweat which can then cause blisters.

Clothing

The next important item for trekking is your clothing. You need reliable clothing that's durable and that you can rely on day-in and day-out. Do not grab your shirts and coats and run out the door. Keep in mind that you need to weather protect yourself while keeping up the pace with the activities required for trekking. Luckily I have learned a thing or two about clothing needed for such adventures. Breathable fabrics and layering is the key. Breathable fabrics are specialized materials that act as a valve between your body and outside weather elements. It stops weather elements from coming in while letting your sweat out at the same time. This feature enables you to perform better. If sweat on your body cannot evaporate, it can make your body overheat or it can get your clothing wet and risk hypothermia. Layering helps you control the temperature that gets to your body. If you are feeling cold, then add additional layer of clothing. When feeling warmer, then take off one layer at a time. Always wear long sleeves as they protect your arms from the sun. At these elevations, the sun is very intense, even though the weather might be quite cold. Layering for cold weather starts with a breathable base layer, then a breathable fleece or windbreaker, and then a layer of outer breathable jacket known as a shell. For warmer weather, you can start with long sleeve breathable shirt and keep a breathable windbreaker handy.

With all that in mind, I went to the Marmot store in San

Francisco and got the base layers, long sleeve shirts, fleece and an outer shell. From the North Face store right across the Marmot store, I grabbed waterproof pants. The Marmot associate was very knowledgeable and knew about layering, and his tips and advice really helped me. While shopping between stores and completing my checklist, I felt blessed to afford such quality clothing equipment with so many selections to choose from. If I were in Pakistan, it would just be a dream.

Look for words such as "wicking", "performance", and "breathable" when shopping for fabrics. In order to stand out, some brands have specific names for such clothing. For example, Nike calls their breathable fabrics as Dri-fit; North Face name them as DryVent; and Marmot call them DriClime. Read the specifications and invest in quality clothing. These materials last for a long time so spending extra also gives you more mileage, which makes it more cost effective.

Medical Kit

One should never skip out on the medical kit. There are certain mandatory items that one should carry. I also prepared a medical kit in which I had moleskin for blisters, painkillers for fever and aches, calamine lotion for skin rashes and insect bites, bandages for cuts, and abrasions, antiseptic wipes to clean wounds, altitude medicine, anti-diarrheal medicine, Vicks for chest congestion, Neosporin for minor cuts and nasal spray to deal with nose and sinus blockage. I missed bugs spray, and I missed them dearly later on. Water purifiers are a must. I carried Iodines tablets. A single small Iodine tablet can purify 1/2 liter of water. Just pop in an Iodine tablet to your water, wait for half an hour and your water is clean ready. There is some aftertaste, but it is worth the trouble.

Along with the medical kit, I prepared a personal hygiene and grooming kit. I bought handy air travel kit from Walmart for $5. It had small size toothpaste, toothbrush, shaving cream, razor, soap, and shampoo. I added body spray to this kit as I knew I would be sharing a tent with others and body spray would be a lifesaver. I had one more kit prepared for safety and survival. This kit had a compass, a small sharp knife, a whistle, headlamp, area map, and a

GPS watch.

Make sure you are aware of your medical conditions such as heart, asthma, or any other serious condition beforehand. Consult your physician. It is better to try out a hike of ten miles in one go and see how you perform.

Other Equipment

Other necessary items that can have an impact on you trekking and are worth highlighting are a sleeping bag, glacier glasses, and a water bladder.

Sleeping Bag:

The sleeping bag is critical for a good night sleep. Getting the right sleeping bag is hard. Sleeping bags that are warmer are relatively heavier and bulkier. Sleeping bags with light down feathers are the best in my opinion. The lightest and the warmest down feather sleeping bags are usually the most expensive. You can settle down on the mid-level sleeping bag that's suitable for reasonable cold nights. In order to compensate for extremely cold nights you can pack a sleeping bag liner. A sleeping bag liner is a sack that can go inside a sleeping bag and can add an extra warmth of 10-30 degrees Fahrenheit. Sleeping bag liners can also act as an inner cover for your sleeping bag and can keep your sleeping bag cleaner as an added benefit. Also, you can always layer up if your sleeping bag is not warm enough for you. I would recommend good warm base layers for a good sleep. Jackets, fleece, and other clothing can provide extra warmth but could be a hindrance between you and a good sleep. I would recommend not to break your bank on the sleeping bag but also don't go cheap on it. Try sleeping bags from good brands, i.e., North Face, REI, Marmot and Mountain Hardware, etc., and buy them from stores that have good return policies. Do read the reviews online but do not get consumed by them and don't be shy about asking questions.

Glacier Glasses:

Glacier glasses are the most often overlooked item for the

Concordia trek, which is mostly glacier trekking. I didn't see anybody other than foreign trekkers carrying glacier glasses on the trek. Glacier glasses are UV (Ultraviolet rays) protected and cover your eyes from sides, top and bottom. Sometimes people confuse glacier glasses with polarized lenses available in the market. Polarized glasses eliminate glare while UV glasses protect eyes from rays that can damage eyesight. Think it of this way; polarized glasses provide some basic protection, but UV provide full protection. Some glasses are both polarized, and UV protected but if your glasses manufacturer doesn't mention UV specifically on the glasses then assume your glasses are not UV protected. Real glacier glasses start from $100 and go up. Julbo is a well reputable brand specializing in glacier glasses. It's worth investing in glacier glasses and if you think you wouldn't need them often then try borrowing from a friend if you can, but do not omit them for your glacier trekking. A good friend of mine suffered snow blindness on a glacier trek once, and it got him scared for his eyesight. It took him some time, but he eventually recovered. He invested in good glacier glasses afterward.

Water Bladder:

There is also one overlooked item; a water bladder. The water bladder is a refillable thick plastic bag with a pipe and a nozzle at one end. A water bladder can be put in your backpack, and the pipe from the water bladder can conveniently provide constant water supply during your hike. These days, backpacks usually have a special pocket for a water bladder and an outlet for the water bladder pipe. The beauty of the water bladder is that you don't have to take water breaks to sip on water. Usually, during the trekking, most of us don't drink water until we take a break. Though it works, we tend to forget as we want to keep our momentum. For longer trekking, dehydration can quickly creep up on you. With a water bladder in your backpack and a nozzle readily available for a sip, you can remain conveniently hydrated while maintaining your momentum. Keep a water bottle as a backup, though. CamelBak makes a good quality bladder. I think it's worth investing in them. There are chances of bladder leaks while on the trek, especially long treks, so a good water bladder is strongly recommended. It is not worth saving money on a water bladder.

Travel Insurance and Satellite Phone

A helicopter rescue at Concordia trek could cost $8,000 to $10,000 and requires an advance deposit. A rescue is perilous and weather dependent. People have to risk their lives for the rescue so rescue may not be guaranteed. You need to deposit the amount before embarking on the journey. If no rescue was needed, then you would get your money back upon your return. There are no signals on the trek, and the only way to connect to the outside world or even call for rescue is via a satellite phone. Investing in satellite phone or making sure your team has a working satellite phone is vital to survival in Concordia emergency situations.

The Concordia area is close to India and China and due to the current geopolitical tensions in the region, your satellite phone purchased or activated outside of Pakistan may not be welcomed there. You might need to secure a satellite phone once in Pakistan through the local telco companies in Islamabad. If you are relying on your team's satellite phone then insist on making a test call. There may be some resistance, but it will be totally worth it, trust me.

Do get yourself travel insurance which includes rescue, hospitalization, change of flights, etc. at the minimum. From the U.S., I have heard people have taken insurances that cost them $350 or up and were worth the expense. The insurance would depend on your country of origin but do your homework and read the fine print and pray that you won't have to make a claim. I didn't take insurance, but when I saw a guy fell right in front of me, I realized the importance of rescue insurance, a satellite phone, and travel insurance. The guy fell 100 feet and fractured his skull. A satellite phone call and on time helicopter rescue saved the man's life. Otherwise, we would have just sat by him and watched him slip away.

APPENDIX C

TREKKING TIPS

Pre-Trekking

1. Do practice hikes with a loaded backpack. Break in or test out your shoes and other equipment. Do not bring brand new or untested items to trekking.
2. Read up on the trek and talk to people who have already done it.
3. Arrange permits, a visa if needed, and other travel documents.
4. Let your loved ones know of your plans, your itinerary, and your trek information. Let them know when you would contact them. Share your tour operator number with them.
5. Create an itemized checklist and work diligently on it.

During-Trekking

1. Carry plenty of water even if you are told you need less water or none. Wear plenty of sunscreen. Wear a hat all the time. Wear full sleeve moisture wicking shirts.
2. Start slow, find your rhythm, and maintain your momentum. Don't rush.

3. Take firm steps, take the lead from porters, observe their stepping and follow.

4. Follow your guide's instructions carefully. Concordia Trek is a glacier trek, and lot of changes happen over a small period.

5. Uphill trekker has the right of way. Make room for trekker from opposite direction if you are descending.

6. Carry out your trash with you. There are trash bins at each campsite, and you can dispose of your waste there. Don't just throw your wrappers or trash on a trek or on the glacier.

7. Keep hydrated. Keep drinking water periodically even if you don't feel thirsty. A water bladder is better than a water bottle.

8. Buddy up with someone who treks at your pace.

9. In case you think you are lost, look for stacked stones. Rocks stacked in one column will tell you which direction to go. If you don't see the stacked stones then use your whistle to get attention.

10. In case you feel dizzy or weird then rest up. Let your guide or senior porter know. They have local remedies and they can help. They have seen it all.

11. Wear double socks; non-cotton, to avoid blisters. Don't puncture blisters. Use moleskin or bandages to cover blisters and avoid any friction between blisters and shoes. Keep blister dry and let them heal on their own.

12. During the climb, don't overcrowd the fixed ropes. Follow the instructions of your guide. If there is no guide around, then make one senior person a leader and follow him. Test your harness, crampons, and another equipment way before the climb.

After-Trekking

1. Stretch and rest up.

2. Check on your team. Share notes and discuss any issues you or they had.

3. Talk to people at the campsite, including porters and guides, and ask what's worth seeing nearby.

APPENDIX D

ITEM CHECKLIST

Following are the items that I took with me. I hope this list helps you with your adventure. I also tried to explain when you would use an item and why you need it.

Clothing

☐ Head Scarf, cotton preferably

> Use: This simple item comes handy in many situations. Use it as a face mask on jeep rides to avoid dust. Use it to cover your head and neck during hikes to avoid direct sunshine or the light rain. You could wrap tightly around your head to cure headaches. Also, avail it as a quick use towel.
> Recommendations: This item is commonly available in Pakistan. You can get it from Islamabad or Skardu from any clothing store. This scarf is nothing but a large handkerchief. I got mine from Islamabad. I think it cost me Rs 300 (3 USD).

☐ Hiking Trousers; UPF 50+, six pockets/convertible

Use: Hiking trousers are made out of light but rugged water resistant and breathable fabric. Use them for your daily hike. These trousers take all the abuse and keep your trekking comfortable. Convertible trousers can be converted to shorts which can be very good for really warm weather hike or a stroll around the campsite. UPF 50+ helps protect your legs from ultraviolet rays. Multiple pockets will help you securely carry multiple items.

Recommendations: These are very common in the U.S. but not so common in Pakistan. You can good brand of these trousers at North Face, REI, Marmot, and many others. Better to get them from the store and try them on to see if they are comfortable. Online may save you some extra money but the trousers may not fit you correctly. Good trousers run from $50-$80. I bought mine for $60 some ten years ago, and they are still doing great. They are worth the expense. I bought a fresh pair from REI just for the Concordia trek.

☐ Running trousers; light and breathable

Use: Use them daily after your hike is over. They can also act as a backup to your hiking pants.

Recommendations: You can get Nike's Dri-Fit, or North Face or REI's. I used Nike's Dri-Fit which I bought for around $60 from Nike outlet. They also last long and have many uses, so they are also worth the expense.

☐ Waterproof trousers; light, breathable and waterproof.

Use: Wear on top of the pants. Use them when it rains heavy on the trail or use them when trekking or climbing in snow. They should be wearable on top of your hiking pants so that you don't have to change while trekking. Also, make sure they have zips on the side legs so that they are easy to slide on or off without taking off your shoes.

Recommendations: Again, go for a good brand. I used North Face's DryVent waterproof pants. Marmot's PreCip and REI's Talusphere are also good choices. They run for

$80 or more. I was able to get mine for $40 due to a pricing error at the North Face store in San Francisco.

☐   Full sleeves hiking shirts

Use: These are light-weight, full sleeve shirts made out of breathable and moisture wicking fabrics. Use them on your daily hikes and when layering up. Make sure you get full-sleeve shirts as they will protect your arms from the direct sun. Exposure to the direct sun can also dehydrate you faster. If your shirt is UPF 50+, that's a bonus.
Recommendations: Breathable and moisture wicking shirt fabric is a mature technology so you can go with any reasonably reputed brand that fits your budget. You can get them from Nike, Addidas, Under Armor, REI, North Face, Marmot and many other. I picked mine for $50 each from Marmot and North Face, but I have found that the ones that I got for $10-$20 on sale were good too.

☐   Windbreaker/Windproof Jacket

Use: Should be light, water resistant, breathable, and packable. Keep it in your backpack during trekking and use it when there is the wind or you feel little chilly. Water resistant helps you protect against light rain but not heavy rain. Some jackets can be packed in their pocket which makes them very compact for storage. Some have vents under the armpit, and you can unzip those vents when feeling warm during trekking.
Recommendations: I used Marmot's DriClime jacket. I recommend you get a windbreaker from a reputable store rather than online if you are not sure about size and model make of the jacket. You need to make sure the jacket is comfortable and fits you great. The jacket can run easily $100 and above. Again these jackets are worth spending money on it. They have a long life, and will serve you well.

☐   Waterproof jacket

Use: Keep this jacket in your backpack and wear it when it rains. A waterproof jacket has same specs as windproof jackets, but they are good for heavy rain. Waterproof jackets are usually less breathable than windproof jackets, so they are not a replacement for the windproof jackets.

Recommendations: Should be light, breathable, and packable. The good waterproof jacket, which is also breathable, runs for $80 or up. I used Marmot's PreCip, which was $100 but I got it for $50 on sale. I tested the jacket out in the rain while hiking and running. If you don't do regular activities than you can settle on a cheaper waterproof outer shell. But if you are avid runner or hiker than this jacket is worth investing in.

☐ Outer Shell Jacket

Use: You will use it for cold weather climbing, and it will be utilized as an outermost layer for the upper body. These jackets are usually heavier and more rugged than the windbreakers. These jackets can take the beating of the weather and are mostly used in climbing in snow or trekking in harsh weather. They also protect against scratches that you might get if you fall. Because these jackets are heavy, they are not ideal for long trekking in normal weather and are not a replacement for windbreakers.

Recommendations: Should be rugged, breathable, armpit vents, windproof, and waterproof, and preferably made of Gore-Tex material. This item is worth going for a good brand. Look for Gore-Tex logo on fabric. Gore-Tex fabric provides excellent protection against heavy winds and rain while keeping your body breathable. These jackets can be pricey and may run for $200 or up. Try to look for deals online and do read up reviews and if possible try out some jackets on trial hikes. Buy from a store with a good return policy. If you are tight on budget, then skip the windproof and waterproof jacket mentioned above and invest in good outer shell jacket. But do keep in mind that you will have to trek with a heavy jacket for long hours which can become very tiring.

☐ Base layers

> Use: Wear them as the first layer in cold weather trekking or climbing especially on snow. Also use them as sleepwear for cold nights.
>
> Recommendations: Should be light, warm, and breathable wear for the upper and lower body. I used Marmot's base layers: two for upper body and one for lower body. They did pretty well. These base layers start at $40 and could go up to $100 or so.

☐ Sleeping Bag and Sleeping bag liner

> Use: You will be using it every night. Some nights it will be freezing cold so keep a sleeping bag liner handy.
>
> Recommendations: Light and warm I have been using REI's sleeping bags for some time and am pleased with their performance. Whichever sleeping bag you settle on, make sure you have tested it in cold weather before bringing it to Concordia. Good sleeping bags starts $100 and up. I have been able to get really good ones from $50-$80 when on sale. If you are an avid adventurer, then invest in good three seasons sleeping bag.

☐ Gloves, 2 pairs

> Use: One-liner pair and one outer waterproof pair. Liner pair or internal pair will keep your hands warm, and the outer pair will insulate your hands from scratches. You will use them for cold mornings until the sun comes out. Most importantly, you would use them gripping climbing ropes at Gondogoro La.
>
> Recommendations: I used North Face's liner gloves and REI's gloves as an outer waterproof pair. There are no recommendations per se here. Try out different gloves and see which one are good but don't skip on buying these.

☐ Hat

Use: Will be used daily to protect you from direct sunlight. Should have a string to go around the neck to secure it. If it is UPF 50+, then it's great.

Recommendations: I used North Face's DryVent that cost me $25. It was UPF 50+ and was water resistant.

Footwear

☐ Hiking Shoes

Use: Everyday, while trekking on regular trail, glacier trail, snow, sand, boulders, and ice.

Recommendations: I used Solomon's Quest 4D hiking shoes that were $240. They are a little steep price wise, but I do regular hikes so I wanted a shoe that I can rely on for many hikes to come. Here were few things you should keep in mind when shopping for a good hiking shoe.

a) The shoe should have a good grip. Try to stand still on a slope with your shoes on and see how your shoe holds on. Make sure you hold on to a railing or some support when doing this test. Look for Verbatim logo on your shoe sole. Verbatim makes great soles.

b) Get a size bigger than you usually wear, since your feet will swell because of long spells of walking.

c) Get a breathable, waterproof shoe, again look for Gore-Tex logo on the shoe.

d) Get yourself ankle high shoe. Ankle high shoe provides more support for longer hikes.

e) Go for test hikes with your shoes and a loaded backpack.

☐ Liner Socks

Use: Wear them under your wool hiking socks. This doubling up of the socks prevent you from blisters.

Recommendations: It should be breathable, wicking and stretchable I went with REI's EcoMade liner socks $6.25 a pair. Buy any pair of any brand just make sure they are moisture wicking and breathable. Avoid cotton socks.

☐ Wool Socks:

> Use: Wear them on top of liner socks. This prevents you from blisters.
> Recommendations: They should be lightweight moisture wicking with reinforced heels, and toes. I went with REI's Merino Wool hiking socks. Buy any pair of any brand, just make sure they are made of wool and are moisture wicking. Avoid cotton socks.

☐ Sandals/Flip Flops

> Use: Mainly used at the campsite for casual use. Walking around, going to toilets, mess tents, etc. Don't use them for your short hikes.
> Recommendations: Any strong but light flip flops or sandals that can stand the beating of travel will do. Make sure they can handle water pretty well.

Equipment:

☐ Day Backpack

> Use: You will use this on the trail every day to carry items you would need during trekking. Use it to carry water, snacks, camera, batteries, solar panel, medical kit, extra clothing, and sunscreen, etc.
> Recommendations: Should be of 30 liters size, waterproof or rain cover, lightweight with good back support. I used REI's 18 liter Flash Pak, but I found it little tight for the Concordia trek. I would recommend any 30 liters backpack, which should be lightweight, have good back support, have easy access to the items and have water bladder pocket. If you can't get a waterproof backpack, then do get a rain cover for the backpack.

☐ Duffel Bag

Use: Large bag to be carried by porters with your stuff that you will not be carrying in your day pack. It will include your sleeping bag, other clothing, equipment, and other travel items.

Recommendations: I used North Face Base Camp duffel bag which I was able to borrow from a friend. They cost $145 and up. Get a bag that's rugged, relatively lightweight, and preferably waterproof. This bag will be carried by porters, will be thrown around and will be put on jeep roof top and will take the beating of the weather, so do not use a suitcase type bag. Make sure you get a lock for the bag as well. Get a bag that you can use for normal traveling so that you can utilize it on non-trekking trips as well.

☐ Water Bladder and Water Bottles

Use: Use water bladder to get a continuous supply of water during trekking. Keep water bottles for backup or for use at campsites.

Recommendations: I used the CamelBak water bladder and Under Armour water bottle. I bought a good quality CamelBak water bladder seven years ago for $35 and it still rocks. Good quality water bottles run for $15-$30. Do get a reliable bladder and bottle that can take the beating on the trek. Once broken, you will not find a replacement on the trek. You then have to rely on used plastic beverage bottles.

☐ Hiking Poles

Use: Use to balance yourself on the treks. Poles also take on load and can help prevent injuries.

Recommendations: I used Black Diamond poles which I bought for $80 around ten years ago. Good quality poles last a long time. They are also adjustable and have shock absorbers. There are more chances that you will lose your poles rather have them broken. I have seen people use wooden sticks as well, but I would recommend good poles for the Concordia trek for your safety. You can use your poles and a large piece of tarp/cloth to make a shade or makeshift tent if needed.

☐ LED Headlamp

Use: You will use it in the night in camp or around the campsite. Also needed when hiking in the night and climbing Gondogoro La at night. The headlamp is preferred over a flash light.
Recommendations: Should be high beam, preferably waterproof. I have used Black Diamond and Petzl headlamps that I bought for $30 each. I have also bought cheap ones, but they don't last more than one trip, and in some cases, they didn't last for more than one day. I would recommend you get a decent one. If it fails during the trek, then it could put you in danger, especially on Gondogoro night climb. If your budget allows, you should get a waterproof headlamp. It could snow or rain, so this will help.

☐ Glacier Sunglasses

Use: Use them when trekking on glaciers and on your Gondogoro La climb. Even if the glaciers are covered with boulders and sand, do use sunglasses. UV rays are stronger in Concordia area.
Recommendations: I used Julbo glasses that I was able to borrow from a friend. They cost $100 and up. Skipping on glacier glasses can harm your eyes, so don't skip on them. These glasses should be UV protected and should fully cover your eyes and the sides.

☐ Solar Panel Charger and Portable Charger

Use: Use it to charge your cameras, cell phone, and portable power bank while on the trek. Keep it optional if your group carry a generator.
Recommendations: I used Anker's 15W USB Solar Charger and Anker's 20000mAh Portable Charger. Each item cost $40. It was helpful in most cases, but since our

team carried a generator, these items were not a deal breaker. But I do foresee using the Solar panel on other trips, so I was good.

☐ Waterproof Pouch

Use: Use it to store items such as cash, passport/identity cards, cell phone, and batteries and to prevent against rain, etc.

Recommendations: I got a waterproof pouch from eBay for $5. I put my identity cards and emergency cash in it and put it in the locked duffel bag that porters carried.

☐ GPS watch

Use: Use it to track your progress, elevation and mileage for your records.

Recommendations: Should be waterproof with good battery life. I used Garmin's Vivoactive HR which cost me $250. This is an optional item but if you intend to buy one then get only reliable waterproof with good battery life.

Miscellaneous Items

☐ Sunblock Cream and Lip Balm

Use: Use daily before the start of the trek or when felt needed.

Recommendations: Get good sunblock and lip balm and carry extra. I bought them from Costco (a popular warehouse store in US) in bulk and took all of them with me. I think it was $10-$15. Make sure they are UPF50+.

☐ Iodine Water Treatment Tablets

Use: Drop in 2 tablets, or as directed by the tablet manufacturer, in a water bladder after filling it with non-boiled water. It kills harmful bacteria in water and makes water safe for drinking. There will be some aftertaste, though.

Recommendations: I picked up some unused Iodine tablets from a friend. These tablets are available at medical stores or sports stores and cost around $15.

☐ Paper Note Book/Pen for Notes

Use: To take some notes along the way if you are interested

Recommendations: I end up using Google Keep app on my cell phone for notes taking. Notebook added extra weight.

☐ Knife, whistle, compass and an area map

Use: Keep these items in your day backpack. Use the knife for miscellaneous tasks, such as cutting bandages, opening cans and for your safety. Use the whistle when you are lost. A whistle is simple yet very effective if you need to be rescued. Use a compass and an area map in case you are lost.

Recommendations: I used REI's keychain which had a compass and a thermometer. I attached a small whistle to the keychain. I believe it was $10 or so. I bought a map from Skardu, but it was very high level. No good maps are available in Pakistan so make sure you arrange one before arriving in Pakistan. Alternatively, you can take printouts of Google Maps for the area. Make sure you turn on Terrain option that displays topology and elevation. Search Askole Pakistan and select the area between Askole and Hushe. Also you can find a good map at http://www.cknp.org/cms/treks-valleys/trekking-routes/classic-treks/

☐ Camera

Use: Take pictures and create memories. This is self-explanatory but keep in mind that large bulkier cameras with all their accessories will be a hindrance to your trekking. You have to balance your needs. You can hand off bulkier camera and accessories to the porter, but you will only get them when back at the campsites.

Recommendations: I took GoPro's Hero Session along with its mount with me. It is light and waterproof. Its wide angle lens creates good panoramic pictures. It cost me $250. Professional cameras with decent lens capture out-of-the-world pictures but then again it's your call. I used GoPro selfie sticks to make POV (Point of View) videos which turned out pretty good for my needs.

☐ Extra Batteries

Use: For camera and headlamp. Keep extra batteries in case your batteries die on you. Keep them in a warm and dry place. Batteries drain very fast on high altitude and colder temperatures, so keep that in mind.
Recommendations: I packed extra AA's and AAA's batteries and snuggled them in the warm clothes.

☐ Toiletries

Use: Small towel, toothbrush, toothpaste, soap, and shampoo. You will use these items at the campsite but not during trekking, so you can pack those items in your duffel bag carried by porters.
Recommendations: I grabbed a travel kit for $5 from Walmart. This came in handy for air travel as well as they were in small quantity. Use your discretion but don't miss out on these basics.

☐ Trail Mix: Dry Fruit/Dates

Use: Use them as a snack during your trekking and climb.
Recommendations: I grabbed trail mix from Costco for $15 that has nuts, almonds, cashews, raisins and M&M's. It was a large pack, and I was able to consume it all the way to the end. And I did share it with my team and others. I am personally not a fan of energy bars, but it is your discretion what you carry as your snack but make sure it

can replenish your energy. Avoid processed food items especially with HFCS (High Fructose Corn Syrup).

☐ Kindle/Books

Use: Read your favorite book when you have free time at the campsite.
Recommendations: I didn't take Kindle and books even though I wanted to. I loaded some audio books on my cell phone however I spent most of the time talking to people and enjoying the scenery.

Climbing Equipment for Gondogoro La:

These items are required if you are planning to do Gondogoro La in addition to Concordia.

☐ Gaiters

Use: Use them when you start your climb for Gondogoro La from Ali Camp onwards. Gaiters prevent snow getting into your shoes.
Recommendations: I borrowed them from a friend of mine. You can rent them from Skardu if you don't do much snow trekking or climbing. Good brand gaiters run for $40 and up.

☐ Helmet

Use: Use it during a climb of Gondogoro La. It prevents head injury in case of rock fall.
Recommendations: I skipped on this to avoid logistics, but I shouldn't have. Good brand helmets start $60 and up.

☐ Harness and Carabiner

Use: You will use a harness to attach yourself to the ropes while doing Gondogoro La climb and descent.

Recommendations: Black Diamond is a decent brand, and their harness is $50 and up and the carabiner is $10 and up. I borrowed from a friend. You can rent from your local sports shop. This is also available for rent from Skardu.

☐ Crampons

Use: Use them on your shoes to get a good grip on snow/ice while climbing Gondogoro La. You will need them after Muneer Camp and may have to take them off before descent if no snow on the descent.

Recommendations: Black Diamond is a decent brand and their crampons are $100 and up. I borrowed from a friend. You can rent from your local sports shop. This is also available for rent from Skardu.

ABOUT THE AUTHOR

The author is your next door guy who has a restless soul that finds solace in nature. The author makes his living as an Information Technology specialist, databases to be relatively accurate, in the Silicon Valley. Originally from a humble Sufi town Multan of Pakistan, the author now calls California his home. The author can be found running in the regional parks of San Francisco suburbs, attending geek sessions at the Silicon Valley tech giants, volunteering at non-profits, solving database problems for tech companies, and hauling his kids to soccer and football practices. Yes, soccer and football are two different sports in the U.S.

24375351R00130

Made in the USA
Columbia, SC
22 August 2018